The
MET & GC JOINT LINE
AN OBSERVER'S NOTES
1948–68

THE MAIN LINE FACE OF LONDON TRANSPORT

The splendid and unique sign at Willesden Green goods yard still in place on 18th. May 1966, some five months after closure. The ex-goods and weighbridge office had since been repainted in a one-off blue and grey scheme.

Thirty-eight miles from the capital, an LT engineer's train hauled by pannier No. L.94 returns to London past Aylesbury South box on 9th. September 1966, six days after the closure of the GC line and the withdrawal of all local BR steam trains.

The
MET & GC JOINT LINE
AN OBSERVER'S NOTES
1948–68

by

Albin J. Reed

Dedicated to the Memory of Bill Wyatt

ACKNOWLEDGEMENTS

My thanks are due to Cllr. Stuart Allen whose father worked on the Met. & GC, Mr. Roy Norris who drove steam and diesel trains on the line, and local historian Mr. Alan Dell for reading the script and making valuable suggestions. I would also like to thank other photographers who have allowed me to use their work. They are named in the captions.

The right of Albin J. Reed to be identified as the Author of the Work has been asserted by him in accordance with the Copyright, Designs and Patents Act 1988.

This book has been sold subject to the condition that it shall not, by way of trade or otherwise, be lent, re-sold, hired out, photocopied or held in any retrieval system, or otherwise circulated without the publisher's consent in any form of binding or cover other than in which this is published and without a similar condition including this condition being imposed on the subsequent purchaser.

Cover illustration by Albin J. Reed
Book production by The Peterhouse Press, Brill, Aylesbury, Bucks
Typeset in Sabon by Avocet Typeset,
Brill, Aylesbury, Bucks
Printed and bound in the U.K. by St. Edmundsbury Press,
Bury St. Edmunds, Suffolk

First Published 1997 by Avon Books Limited
This revised edition privately published in 2001 by Albin J. Reed,
Stoke Mandeville, Aylesbury, Bucks

© Albin J. Reed

ISBN 0 9536252 4 9

CONTENTS

PART 1. HARROW-ON-THE-HILL TO VERNEY JUNCTION:
a general description of the line, its trains and liveries ... 7

Harrow-on-the-Hill to Verney Junction photographs ... 41

PART 2. STOKE MANDEVILLE: A Met. & GC station in detail ... 125

Stoke Mandeville photographs ... 133

APPENDIX 1. Ephemera ... 152

APPENDIX 2. Some Metropolitan Railway numerals ... 156

One on the floor: GWR 2-6-2T No. 6141 is derailed near Hartwell Siding at Aylesbury Met. & GC and GW & GC station on 24th. July 1946. The Slough Loco Dept. breakdown van No. 131 is brown with red ends. The 6100 tanks had been the standard type on GWR trains for many years (apart from on local trains where smaller tanks were used) and they would continue thus until the end of steam.

PREFACE TO THE SECOND EDITION

At the time the first edition of this book appeared I produced a series of booklets also dealing with the Met. & GC Line in whole or in part, and some of the material in them has been incorporated in this new edition. All the photographs are my own work except where otherwise stated.

The entrance to the coal and parcels sidings, Aylesbury Town. 1st. August 1965.

PART 1

HARROW-ON-THE-HILL TO VERNEY JUNCTION

A GENERAL DESCRIPTION OF THE LINE, ITS TRAINS AND LIVERIES

Met. & GC Joint Line

Legend:
- ■■■ MET. & GC JOINT LINE
- —— OTHER LINES
- MET. & GC AND OTHER STATIONS DEALT WITH IN TEXT
- ■□ PASSENGER & GOODS
- ■ PASSENGER ONLY
- □ GOODS ONLY
- ● OTHER STATIONS SOME REFERRED TO IN TEXT
- ■● Stn. closed during 1948–68 period

Abbreviations:
- WH = W. Harrow
- RM = Ruislip Manor
- I = Ickenham

Stations (north from Baker Street / Marylebone):

- Baker Street
- Marylebone
- Finchley Road
- West Hampstead
- Kilburn
- WILLESDEN GREEN
- Dollis Hill
- NEASDEN — NEASDEN DEPOT
- Wembley Park
- Preston Road
- Northwick Park
- HARROW-ON-THE-HILL
- GASWORKS SIDING
- NORTH HARROW
- WH — Rayners Lane — Eastcote — RM — Ruislip — I — Hillingdon — Uxbridge
- PINNER
- NORTHWOOD HILLS
- TIP SIDING
- NORTHWOOD
- WATFORD
- MOOR PARK
- RICKMANSWORTH
- CROXLEY
- CHORLEY WOOD
- CHALFONT AND LATIMER
- CHESHAM
- AMERSHAM
- GREAT MISSENDEN
- WENDOVER
- HALTON CAMP
- STOKE MANDEVILLE
- → To Princes Risborough
- AYLESBURY
- COAL CONCENTRATION DEPOT
- INTERNATIONAL ALLOYS SIDING
- QUAINTON ROAD
- To Bletchley ← Swanbourne → To Oxford
- VERNEY JUNCTION — To the North

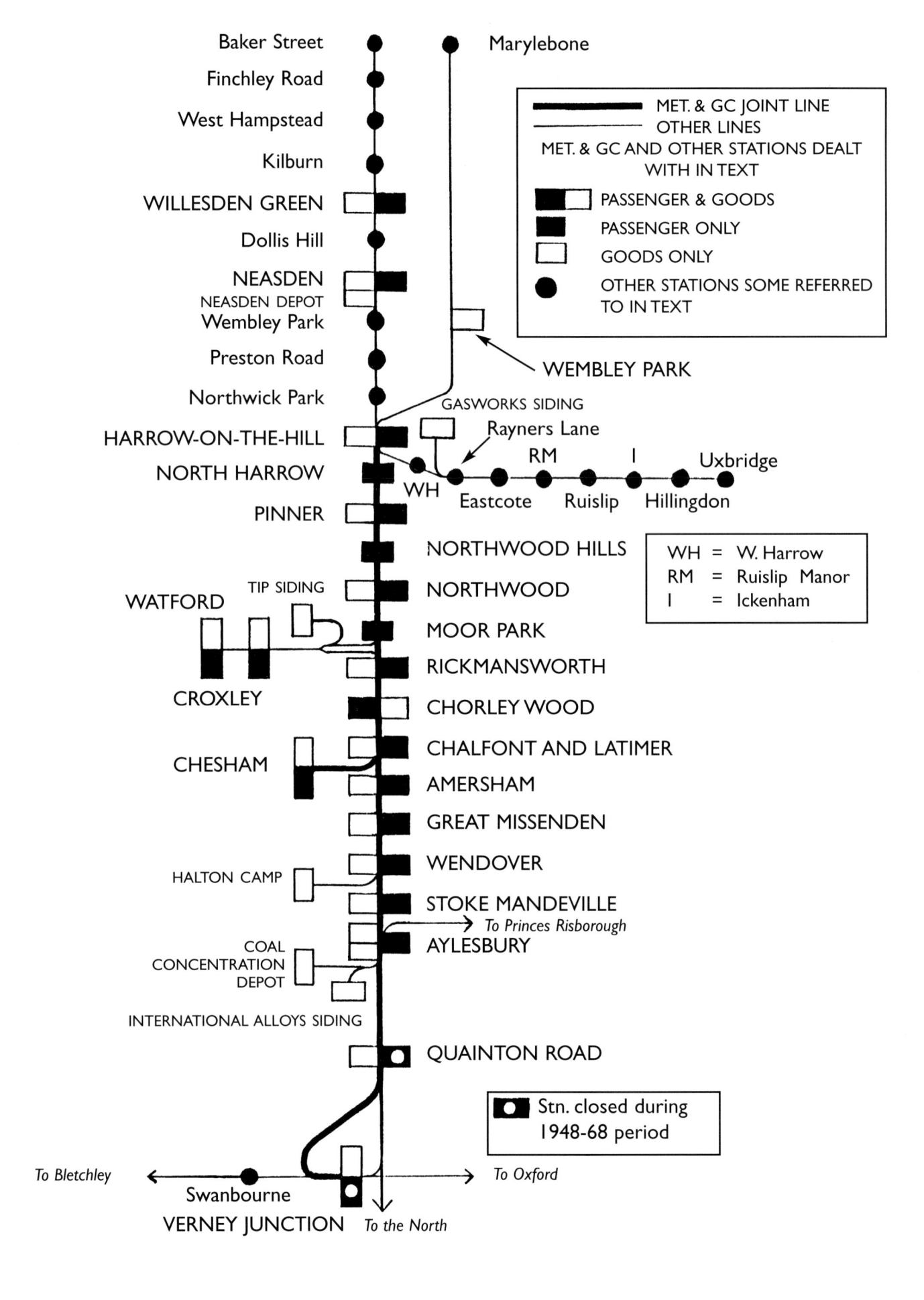

8

GENERAL INTRODUCTION

For forty years I commuted between Aylesbury and Harrow-on-the Hill, during which time I took hundreds of snapshots and made copious notes on the railway scene. From them I have compiled this book, which I offer in the hope that it may suggest a few lines of research to the serious student of the line. I have concentrated on an aspect of the subject that has received less coverage hitherto: colour-schemes and liveries, so the book may also be of interest to modellers. The material is biased towards steam days, the unusual and the 'real railway' side of the line; there is less attention to the diesel era. There are twice as many photographs of the 'linescape' – stations, signs and signals – as there are of trains. I have neither kept strictly within the confines of the 1948-1968 period, nor to the geographical boundaries of Met. & GC territory; where 'real railway' interest existed outside those bounds I have included it.

It may seem rather obvious to state that I have only dealt with what I have seen, and much has gone unrecorded. Some types of engine are not mentioned – for instance I never saw a B16 4-6-0 or an LMS Pacific although they are known to have passed over the line. I hope that readers find herein something to interest them. Their comments or criticisms would be welcome.

ALBIN J. REED
8 Brudenell Drive
Stoke Mandeville
Aylesbury
Bucks
HP22 5UR
November 2000

A last-day ticket from the Oxford-Bletchley line, issued 30th. December 1967.

INTRODUCTION TO THE LINE

From 1906 to 1923 the Met. and GC was a partnership between the GCR and the smaller ambitious Metropolitan Railway, and for the following ten years between the Met. and the LNER. The Met. was itself taken over by the newly formed London Transport in 1933; thus the LPTB and the LNER were the partners in the Met. & GC until 1948. After LT's formation it became clear that the emphasis would be on the second word of the new organisation's title – London PASSENGER Transport Board. Gradually the main line features of its railways – some quite large steam locos, long country routes, goods, parcels and even Pullman car services were to disappear or be greatly reduced. Thus by the time of nationalisation the two partners in the joint committee were two vastly differing concerns. In 1948 when the committee ceased to control the line, most of it was taken over by LT, despite its attempt to rid itself of main line responsibilities. The resulting ex-Metropolitan and Great Central line became full of interest for an enthusiast, both as regards trains and 'linescape'.

Although no part of the Baker Street-Harrow-Verney Junction railway was officially a joint line after nationalisation it still exhibited some of the characteristics of one. For the first few months LT and BR passenger trains shared the tracks not only from Harrow to Aylesbury, but on to Quainton Road too, as correctly shown on the route diagram from a 1948 Eastern Region timetable booklet [A]*. In the sixties LT and BR maintenance trains could sometimes be seen on adjacent tracks, and at that time two BR coal trains began running to Willesden Green goods yard each evening. Before 1962 the service to that depot had consisted of just a few wagons hauled by an LT steam locomotive, but the new arrangements meant that this 'purely' LT depot now had a joint atmosphere. Some of the fuel the BR trains conveyed was destined for a Barnet hospital, and the service was one of the last freight runs on the line. Willesden Green had always retained a main line atmosphere, and even in the 60's the goods office there was stocked with forms to cater for various 'real railway' traffics. They could have sent you a notice of the arrival of compressed gases (see [B]) on a yellow form, or of the arrival of dangerous, corrosive or poisonous chemicals (green), or of gunpowder (pink). There were also blue consignment notes for the carriage of inflammable liquids. Even LT passenger trains from Baker Street shared the 'main line' work, as they carried newspapers [C].

As late as 1981 LT and BR acknowledged the joint nature of the line in print when they distributed a 'leaves on the line' message on the trains (shown at [D]). Finally, [E] is a despatch note received by the author when he purchased a platform oil lamp in 1958 – for two shillings and sixpence (12½p).

Truly a fascinating line!

*Ephemera referred to above are illustrated in Appendix 1.

AN OUTLINE OF PASSENGER SERVICES

So many excellent books dealing with the trains over the former joint lines have been produced during recent years that only the barest sketch of services is called for. The trains of London Transport and British Railways shared the twin tracks from Harrow-on-the-Hill to Quainton Road, the most frequent passenger service being provided by the LT trains from the City or Baker Street which called at Finchley Road, usually at Harrow, then at Moor Park and all stations to Aylesbury. At Rickmansworth, the electric locomotive that had drawn the train from London was exchanged for a BR steam engine in a very swift operation. A typical train on the Watford line would be an electric of T stock, while most Chesham branch trains were formed of ancient Ashbury coaches giving a shuttle service to Chalfont and Latimer; there were through trains in addition.

BR's contribution to the line's services comprised several express trains – some named – from Marylebone to the north, and at the other extreme of speed were the local trains to Aylesbury, Brackley, Woodford or even Leicester. Local folk knew that these trains were the ones to avoid unless one had time to kill! In between were semi-fasts calling at or omitting a variety of stations to Aylesbury and beyond.

The greatest changes to the pattern of services followed the Met. Line modernisation, when tracks were quadrupled to Moor Park and electrified out as far as Amersham. The Met. services to that station and Chesham were thereafter in the hands of electric trains of A stock, and the Met. trains hitherto running to Aylesbury were replaced by BR diesel multiple-units. Initially these ran between Amersham and Aylesbury only, involving a change of train, but after a year or so the full Aylesbury – Marylebone service was inaugurated. Meanwhile the BR steam stopping trains continued to run beyond Aylesbury, as did the 'expresses' which were curtailed at Nottingham; most of these remained steam until the end. The end for these last-named two services came in 1963 and 1966 respectively. Aylesbury was thus the terminus for passenger trains from that time on.

A GENERAL IMPRESSION OF THE LINE IN 1948

Apart from Harrow-on-the-Hill station which had been rebuilt just before the war, little was to be seen of London Transport's fine modern architecture; the line gave the impression that few new buildings had been constructed for many years. The stations were mainly of Metropolitan design, exceptions being the LNER station at Aylesbury and that at Verney Junction on the LMS line. A few air-raid shelters had been converted into huts and fitted with windows (e.g., at Aylesbury and Rickmansworth), and London Transport also made use of wooden huts which were little more than garden sheds. Despite their humble appearance they were well-maintained and creosoted and some had neat rectangular door-plates painted white and lettered in black. Examples were the goods agent's office at Neasden station goods yard, and a p.w. hut at Stoke Mandeville.

Signals, paintwork and details on the northern half of the line differed from those on the southern as the line had been divided for maintenance between the Met./LPTB and the GCR/LNER. The point of division was at Milepost 28½ south of Great Missenden, immediately behind which stood a diamond-shaped board mounted on a short post bearing screwed-on letters reading "DIVISION OF MAINTENANCE MET RY GC RY". Stations on the southern part of the line were in LT colours and exhibited a variety of Met. Railway nameboards of different vintages. Metropolitan semaphore signals were almost universal at the Amersham end of LT territory and were to be seen as far south as Pinner especially at goods yards although colour-lights were in use on the main line.

North of the maintenance division where the LNER had been in charge, nearly all buildings and posts (of signs, signals etc.) still had a drab coat of wartime grey. It was relieved by a little black on signs and post-bases. Signals were in the main GC with a few LNER replacements. Metropolitan survivals could be counted on the fingers of one hand.

THE AYLESBURY LINE GOODS SERVICE

Before 1933 the goods service over the joint lines had been provided by the Metropolitan, and after the formation of the London Passenger Transport Board the goods trains were still hauled by LT locos as successors to the Met. until 1937. All the larger LT locos were then transferred to the LNER which took over the haulage of the goods and passenger trains north of Rickmansworth. These arrangements continued after nationalisation, although it was announced in the national press that "the limited amount of goods now handled (by the LPTB) on the outer sections of the Metropolitan

Line will be transferred to the Railway Executive". Nevertheless the trains providing the ex-Met. goods service continued to appear in the LT Metropolitan Line working timetable as a self-contained group; they were numbered from 1 to about 15. Longer distance BR goods trains running over the ex-Met. & GC lines were not numbered but were merely labelled ER or LMR trains according to period. Conversely, in British Railways timetables their own trains were numbered in a separate series, and the ex-Met. trains were clearly marked "LT".

In the mid-fifties, one 'purely' BR train did operate within the confines of the old Met. & GC system – the 2.10 a.m. from Quainton Road to Harrow; it was shown in the LT and BR timetables as quoted below – one of the ex-Met. trains on the same route is given for comparison:

Train	Shown in LT Timetable as	Shown in BR Timetable as
2.10a.m. Quainton Road to Harrow	E R	1007
10.35p.m. Quainton Road to Harrow	7	10.35p.m. LT from Quainton Road – 7

These arrangements continued until the June 1962 working timetables were introduced, when the ex-Met. goods trains were finally numbered with BR's trains in the four-character system, e.g., 9T06. Besides the main ex-Met. Harrow-on-the-Hill to Quainton Road service, goods trains ran over the Uxbridge and Watford lines and the Chesham branch, and from Harrow southwards to Neasden LT depot, Neasden station goods yard and Willesden Green. They served the South Harrow Gasworks sidings via Rayners Lane. The service from Neasden LT to Willesden Green was in the author's opinion a remarkable survival and will be dealt with at length separately. By 1950, no reference was made in the LT working timetables to any goods working south of Willesden Green; the former exchange sidings with the Midland at Finchley Road were severed in 1953.

There follows a summary of the ex-Met. goods service over the former joint line as it was in Summer 1953. The table shows only trains that ran every weekday or most weekdays – weekend trains are not shown. The pattern remained much the same until the sixties when there was a gradual reduction; in 1964 there were still nine trains over the line; the next year about five; one less in 1966; only two in 1967 and no freight south of Aylesbury in 1968.

SUMMARY OF THE FREIGHT SERVICE IN THE LT WORKING TIMETABLE FOR SUMMER 1953:

TRAIN No.   ROUTE
1. N(BR)-HH-N(LT)-HH-C+L and all goods yards to Ay.
2. HH-Wtfd-Rk-CW-Am-GM-Ay-QR and all goods yards to GM-Rk-HH
3. HH-N(LT)-HH-Ay-QR and all goods yards to Rk-N(LT)-HH-N(BR)
4. N(BR)-HH-N(LT) (Tues. & Thurs.)
5. N(LT)-Ay-QR-Ay-Rk-Wtfd-Cx-Nwd-P-HH
6. HH-E-Hill-Ux-R-HH
7. HH-GM-Ay-QR-Ay-HH
8. HH-RL-Gas-RL-HH
9. N(LT)-WG-N(LT)
10. Ay-QR-Alloys-Ay-QR-Ay-GM-HH-N(LT)
11. HH-N (LT)-HH

12. C+L-Ay
13. C+L-Cm
14. Cm-C+L
15. HH-Hill-Ux-HH

This timetable also includes these trains which are not numbered:

Eastern Region
N(BR)-Woodford
Woodford-Ay-N(BR)
Woodford-Ay-N(BR)
N(BR)-Ay-Woodford
Woodford-QR-HH

Western Region
Paddington-Ay-Princes Risborough
Princes Risborough-Ay-Paddington

An earlier timetable (1950) also gives
London Midland Region
Swanbourne-QR

Key to abbreviations:

N(BR)	Neasden Sidings (BR)	Ux	Uxbridge	Cm	Chesham g.y.
N(LT)	Neasden Yard (LT)	P	Pinner g.y.	Am	Amersham g.y.
WG	Willesden Green g.y.	Nwd	Northwood g.y.	GM	Great Missenden g.y.
HH	Harrow-on-the-Hill g.y.	Cx	Croxley g.y.	Ay	Aylesbury g.y.'s
RL	Rayners Lane g.y.	Wtfd	Watford g.y.	Alloys	International Alloys Siding (Aylesbury)
GAS	Gasworks sidings				
E	Eastcote g.y.	Rk	Rickmansworth g.y.	QR	Quainton Road g.y.
R	Ruislip g.y.	CW	Chorley Wood		
Hill	Hillingdon g.y.	C+L	Chalfont & Latimer g.y.		

N.B. Wendover and Stoke Mandeville goods yards do not feature in the list as they are included in "all goods yards to ..."

TYPES OF STEAM LOCOMOTIVES USED

The locomotives used immediately after nationalisation reflected the LNER's part-ownership of the line. In 1948, ex-GCR Class A5 4-6-2T's were common on Met. and Marylebone commuters' trains, supplemented by the new LNER-designed Class L1 2-6-4T's, still in green but lettered "BRITISH RAILWAYS" in full in yellow. One of them, No. 67720, remained green long enough to receive a lion-and-wheel totem. The surviving ex-Met. Railway 0-6-4T's and 2-6-4T's were also used on both suburban passenger and freight work. Long distance expresses were often in the hands of Class B1 4-6-0's, and A3 Pacifics; V2 2-6-2's were also used. Local goods trains were hauled by ex-GCR L3 2-6-4T's; W.D. 2-8-0's could also be seen and on 27th. June 1951, even an ex-GNR 0-6-0 turned up. Ex-GCR J11 0-6-0's were used on goods, engineer's and even passenger trains. The London Transport Chesham branch trains were mainly hauled (or pushed) by ex-GCR C13 4-4-2T's. These locos were sometimes used on the Met. Line business train leaving Aylesbury soon after 7 a.m., 64720 being a regular performer. Just out of shops in its new BR lined livery in 1950 (on the 10th. January for example), its work was barely distinguishable from that of the larger tanks. Sometimes push-and-pull fitted ex-GCR 0-6-2T No.69257 joined the C 13's. Members of this class did local freight jobs, and the same 69257 was working a trip to Wembley Park ex-Met. yard on 4th. November 1957; on 31st. October 1950 69341 had handled the Harrow Gasworks coal train. N5's also did turns on the Aylesbury to Princes Risborough branch, and this line brought ex-GWR types to Aylesbury – mainly 61XX 2-6-2T's for mixed traffic, various panniers and the small 14XX 0-4-2T's for push-and-pull work.

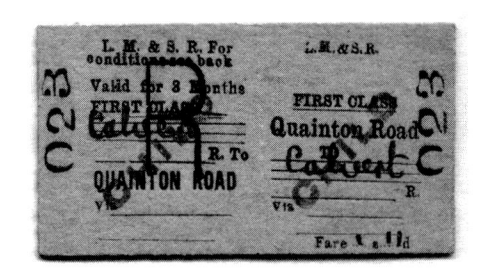

Three tickets issued on the last day that Quainton Road was open, 2nd. March 1963. No. 4964 is almost certainly the last issued *and used* as the author was the only passenger joining the train. Note the "M&GC" and "LMSR" on the other two tickets.

In the later years of steam when the LMR supplied the motive power ex-LMS 2-6-4T's and 'Black Five' 4-6-0's became mainstays on the main line of the old Met. &GC and 'pure' GC routes. Of the BR Standard range of engines, Class 4 2-6-0's became very common particularly on freight trains, especially those which were tripcock-fitted for working over LT lines; they were not unknown on Nottingham trains. Class 4 Standard 2-6-4T's were also used on suburban work, and Class 5 4-6-0's helped out on expresses (and on humbler trains at times). 'Britannia' Pacifics were liable to appear among the Black Fives on Nottingham trains; for instance No .70046 was used on 27th. October 1965. The Class 9 2-10-0 freight locos could be seen on goods work at Aylesbury, and even on the longer distance fast trains, as could ex-LMS named 4-6-0's. Examples are 46156 on the fast Marylebone train calling at Aylesbury at 10.31 a.m. on the 20th. December 1963, and 92021 and 92023 on similar duties on 23rd. and 27th. July 1960.

EXAMPLES OF ENGINES USED ON MET. & GC LINE TRAINS

N.B. "MC" & "EC" refer to the morning and evening Met. commuter trains used by the author between Aylesbury and Harrow-on-the-Hill and return.

DATE	ENGINE CLASS	NUMBER	NOTES ON TRAIN
14-1-48	B 1	61083 & 1185	On 12.59 p.m. XP from Aylesbury to Marylebone.
1-4-48	L 3	E 9068	On local goods.
11-4-48	J 11	–	On p.w. work at Stoke Mandeville.
13-4-48	L 1	E 9005	On Met. passenger duty.
20-4-48	L 3/A 5	69054 & 69827	First two locos seen with 6XXXX numbers.
22-3-48	–	Electric No.9	On the Quainton Road train from Liverpool St.
3-48	L 1		Approx. 30% of Met. trains now hauled by green L1's, renumbering to 6XXXX.
6-6-48	B 1	61028	On 8.20 a.m. Marylebone with 4 corridors.
Mid-49	J 11	64329	On shunting duty at Harrow yard.
21-7-49	A 3	60052	On "Master Cutler" with tavern car "Dolphin".

DATE	ENGINE CLASS	NUMBER	NOTES ON TRAIN
12-9-49	N 7	–	MC – out-of-steam twice.
10-1-50	C 13	67420	MC – frequently used.
"	A 5	69804	EC.
13-1-50	C 13	67438	EC.
"	L 1	67758	EC.
16-1-50	L 1	67756	EC.
17-1-50	L 1	67760	MC.
18-1-50	A 5	69828	EC.
19-1-50	L 1	67720	EC. Green with totem.
"	B 1	61185	On "South Yorkshireman".
21-1-50	A 3	60061	On semi-fast duty from Aylesbury.
23-1-50	A 5	69805	EC.
24-1-50	A 5	69806	EC.
25-1-50	A 5	69804	MC.
"	A 5	69805	EC.
27-1-50	L 1	67715	EC.
"	L 1	67717	EC.
28-1-50	A 3	60061	On semi-fast duty from Aylesbury.
31-1-50	14 XX	1411	On P. Risborough push-and-pull to Aylesbury,
"	L 1	67752	EC.
4-2-50	A 3	60111	On 10.0 a.m. ex-Marylebone. Blue.
14.2.50	A 5	69821	EC. Very good run.
15-2-50	A 5	"	EC. Very good run.
16-2-50	A 5	69820	On 6.8 p.m. ex-Marylebone to Aylesbury.
17-2-50	B 17	61669	On 7.25 a.m. ex-Aylesbury.
"	L 1	67714	EC.
"	WD	900XX	Derailed whilst shunting in Northwood goods yard.
25-2-50	A 3	60111	On 9.41 a.m. ex-Aylesbury.
5-3-50	B 1	61185	On 9.41 a.m. ex-Aylesbury.
7-3-50	V 2	60818	On "South Yorkshireman".
18-3-50	A 3	60061	On 9.41 a.m. ex-Aylesbury. Loco still green.
3-6-50	A 3	60048	On 9-41 a.m. ex-Aylesbury.
2-10-50	F	L.49	Shunting Neasden station goods yard.
5-1-51	–	Electric No.6	On Chiltern Court Coal Neasden-Baker Street with three wagons and B.572.
1-2-51	N 7	69694	MC. Out-of-steam at Wendover.
6(?)-3-51	N 7	–	MC " "
9-4-51	4	LMS 2-6-4T	MC. 1st. recorded use on this line.
24-6-51	E	L.4X	On Met. passenger duty at Aylesbury.
27-6-51	J11	–	On 5.1 p.m. ex-Marylebone.
8-10-51	E	L.44	On Met. passenger duty at Aylesbury.
26-12-51	B1	61329	On 5.11 p.m. ex-Aylesbury.
2-2-52	A3	60054	On "South Yorkshireman".
21-12-52	E	L.46	On p.w. duty with rail-wagons at Rickmansworth.
21-12-52	F	L.49	On p.w. train with B.567 at Chalfont.
5-1-53	A3	60048	On 1.49 p.m. ex-Marylebone.
7-1-53	F	L. 51	Apparently on standby at Rickmansworth.

Continued overleaf

Continued from previous page

DATE	ENGINE CLASS	ENGINE NUMBER	NOTES ON TRAIN
13-8-54	A3	60049	On "South Yorkshireman".
22-3-55	4	42239	MC. Out-of-steam for 30 mins. at Great Missenden.
25-8-55	A3	60052	On 2.30 p.m. ex-Aylesbury.
8-1-56	V2	60815	On 6 suburban coaches on 8.05p.m. ex-Marylebone – very early.
28-1-56	A3	60062	On 10 a.m. ex-Marylebone.
31-3-56	V2	60980	On "Master Cutler".
27-12-56	B1	61077	On Calvert push-and-pull.
14-7-57	V2	60878	On 3.24 p.m. to Marylebone.
18-3-58	C 13	67420	On Calvert and Princes Risborough trains for several days, very unusual.
23-12-60	B1	61187	On 9.41 a.m. ex-Aylesbury.

THE WILLESDEN GREEN GOODS SERVICE

The freight service from Neasden Depot to Willesden Green was one of the most fascinating of those on the Aylesbury line, as its trains were hauled throughout our period until May 1962 by London Transport steam locomotives, and LT brake vans were often provided.

Several local coal merchants received their supplies at Willesden Green, and they had offices in Station Parade adjoining the yard. Two of the firms told me that the paperwork they handled was headed "London Transport", one of them adding "Metropolitan Line". By 1960, however, a letter from the head office of one of them indicated that as far as they were concerned their traffic was handled by British Railways, London Midland Region. I was told by the station master in 1960 that since 1951 all accounts and working expenses had been charged to Euston.

The single midday train, numbered 9 or 10 in the working timetable, usually consisted of anything up to about fifteen coal trucks, and carried a Class K headlight. On arrival at Willesden Green via the fast Met. road the loco would position the wagons it had brought, collect the empties, remarshal the brake and run round. Work done, it would give a magnificent crow on its whistle as it awaited a path back to Neasden over the local (Bakerloo) road. Besides coal, builder's materials were handled, and Western Region bauxite-painted Hybar and Shocwagons could sometimes be seen being unloaded into a merchant's lorry at the north end of the yard, with the help of small crane C. 610 which was usually stationed there. Tube wagons were occasionally seen on a siding near the entrance where a firm of scaffolders had their premises.

The main building at the yard was an oddly-shaped angular structure shared by merchants, shunter and goods agent. A single storey brick building adjoining and facing the gates served both as weighbridge office and entrance to the inner goods office. Nearer the running lines was the corrugated iron goods shed, which only lasted a few years into the period being described before being demolished. A member of staff told me that a firm of fruiterers wished to use the shed as a banana store, but LT did not approve, so Harrow goods shed was used instead. The platform within, and the main parts of its crane remained in situ until after 1968. The weighbridge existing in 1948 was not used again; the current record book gave entries from 1930 until that date. The forms therein were headed "Metropolitan Railway". I also learned from the station master that the cattle dock, which still existed in 1960, had not been used since 1923 when he took office.

The two small windows of the weighbridge office were replaced by one larger one and a much larger weighbridge was installed in early 1962. Even more surprising was the erection at the same time of a new cedarwood goods office (a garden shed de luxe) on the south end of the former goods shed platform, to which the enamel sign from the old office was transferred. A new London Transport goods office in 1962, cosmetically at least! These works were the prelude to a take-over of the haulage by BR on 7th. May 1962, after which much more coal was handled, particularly for Charringtons who had recently arrived. Up to 60 wagons could be seen in the yard at any one time. Steam traction was soon replaced by diesel, the trains coming either from Neasden BR sidings via Harrow or direct from Quainton Road. Despite the BR take-over of haulage, the LT signs remained unchanged.

All these changes were however overtaken by events in 1966 when the yard was closed, the traffic being transferred to Willesden Junction. During the years that LT steam engines worked the service, every class of locomotive was at some time employed except one which was never seen – the solitary A Class 4-4-0T No. L.45, which had only a few months of active life left in 1948, and which was usually stationed at Lillie Bridge near West Kensington. One unexpected loco from this last-named depot which did appear on Willesden Green goods trains on several occasions however was No. L.30, one of the two Hunslet 0-6-0Ts not normally used in revenue-earning service.

EXAMPLES OF GOODS TRAINS TO WILLESDEN GREEN

DATE	ENGINE	FORMATION, BRAKE-VAN & NOTES
5-1-51	L.48	Approx. 10 wagons and LT brake B. 562.
7-1-52	L.49	Approx. 15 wagons and grey ER brake.
22-12-52	L.51	Approx. 20 wagons and ER brake.
4-8-53	L.53	Approx. 20 wagons and ER brake.
16-8-55	L.53	8 wagons and BR brake.
7-9-56	L.46	7 wagons and B. 573.
4-11-58	L.90	4 wagons, 5 bolster wagons for p.w. dept and BR brake.
30-12-58	L.52	5 wagons and B.553.
8-10-59	L.52	3 wagons and B.572.
5-8-60	L.30	6 wagons and BR brake.
8-8-60	L.30	Approx. 7 wagons and B.554.
27-12-61	L.46	2 rail-wagons, 2 coal and B.553.
8-1-62	L.44	1 wagon and B. 554.
28-2-62	L.95	2 wagons and B.554. Returned with one goods van.
17-5-62	(BR takes over haulage)	

METROPOLITAN LINE TRAINS TO QUAINTON ROAD

By the time of the post-war years, as far as the London public was concerned the Metropolitan Line ended at Aylesbury. It was shown thus on the Underground map and on the maps and diagrams displayed in the steam stock carriages. Yet there were two Met. trains that went beyond Aylesbury to Quainton Road – the 4.53 p.m. from Liverpool Street (5.08 p.m. from Baker Street Saturdays) and the 10.08 p.m. from Baker Street (10.00 Saturdays). The trains did not run on Sundays. The trains were correctly shown on the Train Departures posters at Baker Street, but when the teatime train was observed at this station on 12th. February 1948 it was not shown on the platform indicators as running beyond Aylesbury. The station announcer declared that the next train on Platform 2 would call at "Finchley Road, Moor Park, Rickmansworth, Chorley Wood, Chalfont & Latimer, Amersham,

Great Missenden, Wendover, Stoke Mandeville, Aylesbury and Quainton Road: all stations to Quainton Road and Aylesbury" (note the order). The trains were properly equipped with "QUAINTON ROAD" destination plates, though no doubt passengers at Liverpool Street were puzzled by this destination when they saw the 4.53 waiting to start its 48.35-mile journey! When observed leaving Aylesbury on five occasions during 1948 the early evening train loaded to one passenger each time except once when numbers swelled to five, and once the return working had six people. On two occasions the late-night down train had six passengers each time. A5 (6)9829 provided the motive power on 8th. April 1948 and (6)9805 the next day. In contrast to their progress up the hills from Rickmansworth, beyond Aylesbury they produced some very lively running over the much flatter six miles to Quainton Road.

These interesting workings only lasted some five months under the auspices of the new London Transport Executive however, and the last Met. train ran to Quainton on 29th. May 1948. The curtailment was not over-publicised, and after the train rolled into the bay platform at Aylesbury on one night soon after, some would-be traveller to Quainton was told by a rustic voice booming through the darkness that if he wanted to go to Quainton he'd have to walk ...

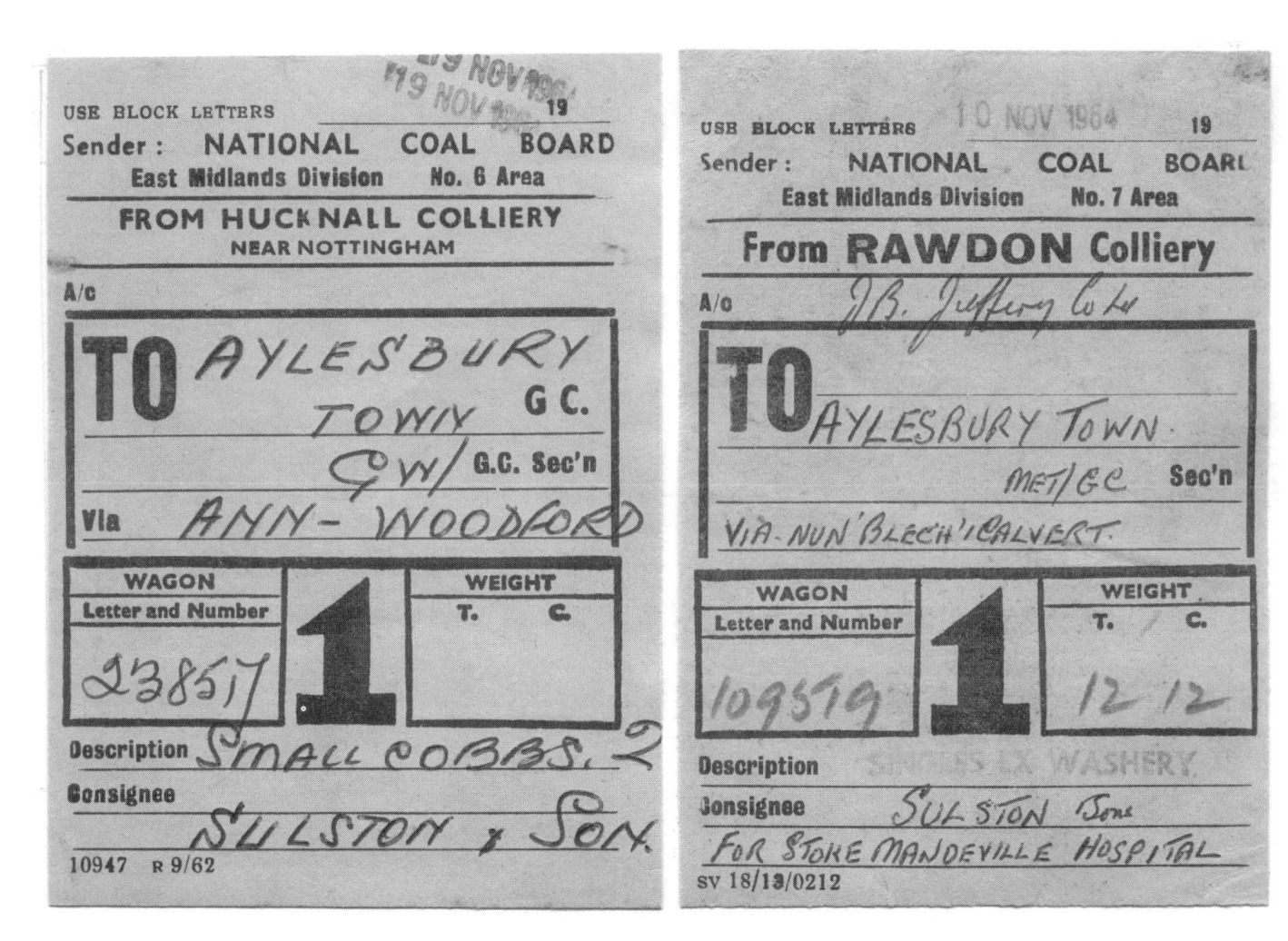

Old railway names die hard: note the "Met./GC and "GW/GC" sections referred to on these 1964 wagon labels. Two other labels had "Met." Section and "GC/MR" Section.

ENGINEER'S TRAINS

Before nationalisation when the division of maintenance was at Great Missenden, the track north thereof was maintained by the LNER. Although LT took over most of the old Met. & GC line in 1948, Eastern Region trains continued to do maintenance work south of Aylesbury well into that year. A typical train would be hauled by an ex-GC J11 "Pom Pom", and would include vehicles in LNER Oxford blue (often faded to cobalt), and some where the initials "GCR" could still be made out underneath the grime. When LT took over in earnest one of its first jobs was to rerail a crippled parcels van near Wendover, to which L.44 brought the breakdown train.

The appearance of LT locos as far north as Aylesbury became a frequent occurrence due to the need to take water, although Aylesbury was strictly off their beat. One day in 1956 this station seemed to have reverted to the heyday of the Met. Railway when, for a short time, every vehicle in sight was LT-owned: rakes of brown steam stock, red-ended goods brakes and an LT steam locomotive. The first pannier used on these trains was ex-GWR 7711, still in plain black livery with old totem. Other panniers, by then in full LT maroon livery, continued to visit Aylesbury after the final withdrawal of BR steam trains in 1966; for instance, L.94 was observed leaving Aylesbury with a short p. way train on 9th. September of that year. These trains were allocated BR-style reporting numbers, e.g., 9Z25.

At this period similar trains on the BR section often had diesel haulage; for example a bank-slip job near Stoke Mandeville Hospital was attended on 25th. July 1965 by trains hauled by D 2510. As on occasion the BR train on this work would be passed by an LT steam train on the other track, the line sometimes had a more 'joint' atmosphere in the sixties than it had ever done in the old company days!

EXAMPLES OF LT ENGINEER'S TRAINS REACHING AYLESBURY

DATE	ENGINE	FORMATION AND NOTES
29-5-50	L.50	Collects crane, 2 wagons & brake.
21-8-55	L.44	Brake, 11 open wagons, B.575.
28-3-56	L.50	B.566, H.W.'s 417, 416, 413, 424, B.573. H.W.417 had hot wheel, so left at Aylesbury.
4-4-56	L.50	B., 5 flat wagons with continuous rail, B.575.
5-4-56	L.51	B., H.W's 400, 410, 413, 4XX, B.
12-4-56	L.50	B.573, 4 H.W.'s, B.
16-4-56	L.52	B.554, HW.400, 3 others, B.563.
"	L.48	Collects 3 damaged Dreadnought coaches with Dreadnought 485 as brake. Class D headlights.
25-5-56	7711	First pannier seen on LT train. B., hopper wagons & B.566.
18-7-65	L.95	B.580, F.347, 336, R.W.455, 489, BR van B 504750, B.585.
25-7-65	L.95	B.567, R.W.454 (old sleepers), 317, P.H.944, B.580. Also BR p.w. train with D2510 on same day.
6-4-66	L.96	B.555, 2 sand wagons, 2 BR vans, B.557.
12-6-66	L.93	B.58X, wagons, B.560. Sleepering at Stoke Mandeville.
19-6-66	L.90	B.584, H.W.'s 426, 416, 413, 426, 411, F.392, 35X, B.555.
24-8-66	L.96	B.581, 5 H.W.'s, B.555. Ballasting at Stoke Mandeville.
25-8-66	PBT.760 Tamping machine	Parked on ex-GW&GC siding (very rare occurrence) for 9 days.
9-9-66	L.94	B.581, H.W.'s 421, 412, 414, B.582. First steam train seen since end of BR steam on this line (3-9-66).
5-10-66	L.93	3 wagons and brake. Last LT steam train observed at Aylesbury.

THE HALTON CAMP BRANCH

The Halton Camp branch was a goods-only line which ran from Wendover goods yard to the RAF workshops on Chestnut Avenue, Halton. It had been opened during the first world war; some of the point-levers were marked "WD 1917". In its heyday it carried 500 tons of coal weekly in addition to other traffic. Originally a steam line, latterly two Air Ministry diesels numbered 223 and 240 (both 0-4-0s) had been in use, and before them an 0-6-0 numbered AMW 188. This loco was painted light olive or sage green, with holly green edging separated by a fine white line. Its frames were black, lined in red. It is almost certain that no passenger train ever used the line. It rarely hit the headlines except, for example, when a BR brake van ran away from Wendover goods yard and derailed itself on (or off) the Halton line near bridge MR 144 on 29th. January 1961. It had to be rescued by a BR crane propelled at the head of a line of wagons, as BR motive power was not allowed on the branch. Conversely, Air Ministry locos were officially prohibited from entering the Wendover goods yard, though I watched one shunting alongside the goods shed on 13th. April 1948 nevertheless.

It may not be widely known that when the line was proposed for closure in March 1963 it was the subject of a preservation scheme considered by the London Underground Railway Society. The author had a preliminary discussion with the Resident Works Engineer on the Society's behalf, but major obstacles led to the idea being abandoned. These included the need for general track renewal, the maintenance of the bridge over the Wendover arm of the canal and the presence of the multi-gate level crossing over the busy A 413 road.

UNUSUAL TRAINS

Well-maintained LNER locos were in short supply after the war and in case of failure an LT E Class loco would be on standby at Rickmansworth in case it were called on to take a passenger train forward. The appearance of a clean, red and gold engine after years of nothing but filthy black ones caused quite a stir among local enthusiasts – in fact it rekindled the author's latent interest in railways after a wartime eclipse by aircraft! These workings continued into 1951 at least.

The Chesham shuttle was quaint enough in itself with its ancient flat-roofed coaches, but when it had an extra engine and a luggage van at the north end, as it did on a regular teatime train in the fifties, the effect was even more remarkable. When, on one occasion the van was replaced by an ex-GC coach, the effect was unique. On another day the van used was an ex-LNER passenger-type van No. E2173E, which, like the GC coach, was still in the mid brown which persisted on older ER stock long after the advent of red BR liveries. On these two occasions the whole train had a decidedly pre-nationalisation air.

Every Sunday morning the two 3-coach Chesham sets were changed over, the retiring set heading quaintly up the main line to Neasden Depot and crossing with the other. On 24th. July 1960 a hitch must have occurred, as the returning set did not head for Neasden straight away but was seen in Chalfont yard with 0-4-4T No. L.44 attached – the only time I saw that combination of LT steam loco and Ashbury coaches. I quickly reached for my camera – and the film jammed: the one that got away!

Another unusual combination that passed my homeward commuters' train regularly for a period in the fifties, often near Chalfont or Chorley Wood, comprised a BR Class L1 2-6-4 tank and a couple of LT goods brake vans, often with an odd wagon too. It was quite common to see LT trains hauled by one of their steam locos with a BR brake, but the above-mentioned train was the only one I ever saw with BR motive power and LT brake(s). The author would welcome information on this train's origin and purpose.

Not so special but decidedly unusual was one of the Met. Line's early morning steam business trains which left Aylesbury on 12th. October 1955 with a brake-third coach at the London end only. The north-end brake, No 496, had been declared unserviceable not long before departure, so the train left with five coaches only and was due to be taken out of service at Wembley Park. This was the only time I saw a train of Dreadnoughts in passenger service with other than six coaches.

THE MET. & GC CRANE

For almost the whole of the period under review there stood on a siding near Harrow goods shed a small crane and jib-wagon which according to a 1954 note of mine, was "used for containers". Cast-iron plates on their solebars indicated that the vehicles together formed "MET. & GC No.1". When first observed both wagons appeared to be blackish, the only lettering being "No.1" on the solebars of the crane truck. Early in 1954 the crane truck reappeared after a short interval away fully repainted in LT colours. Mid grey was the basic colour, with liberal touches of Underground red on the end of the jib, other moving parts and buffer beams. The solebars and underframes were black, and bore the number C. 619 in the LT crane series, the characters being in correct Johnston style. Apart from various legends of instruction and the out-of-date cast plates, there was no other wording. The brake-handle, like the small legends, was painted white.

The jib wagon was also repainted a couple of months later.. The basic scheme was the same, including the red buffer-beams, but the black parts were fewer, the grey extending to the solebars. This wagon was duly numbered in the LT jib wagon series, but besides showing no ownership did not even carry the "J." prefix to the number "690". Some time later (interval unrecorded), the numbers on both vehicles were painted out with white oblongs, leaving them nameless and numberless apart from the small italic legends and the cast plates. There was no other change during the rest of the wagons' stay at Harrow, and it was in the faded remains of the above livery that they arrived at the Bucks Railway Centre.

THE PARCELS SERVICE

Delivery of parcels was made by BR road vans, which on the LT section were driven by LT personnel. In early days after nationalisation these vans retained their LNER livery of dark blue with red wheels, though of course lettered "BRITISH RAILWAYS". An example was EB2324 whose number on the cab door acquired a prominent "E" for Eastern Region. This van, whose registration number was EXR 626, was often seen at Harrow-on-the-Hill. There followed a long period when vans were painted in the simple and pleasing carmine and cream scheme with totems, but unlike rail vehicles in the same colours, were unlined. Less distinctive liveries (e.g., mostly yellow) were adopted in the sixties, but towards the end of the period contractors' lorries were employed, at least on the BR sections of the line. The service disappeared gradually – for instance, between Amersham and Stoke Mandeville it ceased on 18th. April 1966, while at Rickmansworth and Chalfont it lingered on until 3rd. November 1966. Luggage labels were printed with British Railways' initials even on the LT section, for example "BR Chesham".

At the very start of the period a remarkable survival could be seen at Amersham. It was a lorry still in Met. teak livery and lettered "Metro & LNE Railways" in blue-shaded gold letters. Its registration number was in the GT series.

LONDON TRANSPORT RAILWAY LIVERIES

British Railways liveries have been well recorded but a few notes on those of London Transport may not come amiss, particularly as regards those of 'real railway' vehicles taken over from the Metropolitan.

The oldest working LT steam loco in 1948 was Class A 4-4-0T No. L.45 of 1866, and when she was withdrawn a few months later she still bore the paint-date 1/34. She was finished in standard maroon and lined and edged in black and 'imitation gold', i.e. non-metallic gold-colour. The

"LONDON TRANSPORT" legend on her sides was hand-painted in the same shade edged black, the only example I saw before 1968 where the standard gilt transfers were not used. Her Met. number "23" had long been patched over and "L.45" had been applied instead in the same colour. Apart from the lettering, all other LT locos received the same treatment in our period, though the shade of imitation gold varied somewhat; it was sometimes more of a deep cream as on L. 44 compared with the slightly deeper gold-colour on L. 46 when both were compared in 1946. The maroon could vary slightly too, being different in tone or browner than usual. With the advent of the ex-GWR pannier-tanks a new lining colour of light yellow became standard, which was later used on most loco repaints. It was similar to the yellow used on some bus doors and for late Green Line lettering, and did not give the pleasant illusion of being gilt as did the earlier buff.

In 1948 coach livery was absolutely standard: sides of ex-Metropolitan Railway compartment stock were finished in imitation graining representing teak, and all ends were painted warm mid brown. In 1951 however, graining was abandoned and thereafter sides and ends were painted a colour best described as 'tan', a yellowish brown of rather garish shade often shown on shade-cards as golden-brown. No. 436 was the first coach I saw thus finished. This colour wore well and when a little grime had accumulated in the panelling it really did differ little from weathered teak. Before this hue became standard another innovation was made – the ends of brake coaches were painted Underground red. It was applied to all brakes, whether the sides were still grained or in the 'tan' finish. In 1954 a new main body colour was introduced – a slightly darker mid brown best described as 'milk chocolate' colour. It was richer than the tan shade but did not contrast so well with the maroon of the electric locomotives. Brake ends continued to be painted red with the new brown, but it gradually changed to London bus red during our period. Carriage roofs were usually a dull brown but sometimes grey or a near-black was used. Until about 1953 all ex-Met. Railway passenger vehicles bore the LT logo, split into two panels. The vehicle number appeared at each end of each side in the same black-edged gilt. Just before the advent of the mid brown, lettering began to be omitted from all except driving vehicles, and brake-third No. 427 was seen thus unadorned. All repaintings in the final mid brown were also anonymous, except for two 'flashes in the pan' when 446 and 491 (repainted 1/56) reappeared with lettering. The latter was the last Dreadnought ever to be lettered, and happily its finish remained in good condition until the end – in fact it was in the rake of the very last LT passenger train to leave Aylesbury. Apart from the two vehicles just mentioned, the words "LONDON TRANSPORT" could no longer be seen on any steam coaches north of Rickmansworth including the Chesham branch.

LT LIVERY OBSERVATIONS

The following observations of LT liveries were compiled in November 1957, with a few later additions. N.B. 'Johnston' refers to the style of lettering used by LT; it is similar to BR's Gill Sans.

Steam Locomotives
Maroon, including all wheels and inside frames, lined mid yellow/black/mid yellow on tanks (and on sides and rear of bunker on ex-Met. and District Line types). Edging of black/mid yellow on cabs, steps, splashers (and toolboxes etc. where fitted, and on sides and rear of bunker on ex-GWR panniers). Frames lined mid yellow on extreme lower edge of frames. Bufferbeams (unlined), coupling-rods and motion red. Whistle brass, brass beading on splashers on some locos. Standard LT legend in gilt on tank sides, and number on front buffer-beam gilt; side and rear numbers in lining yellow.

Coaches (ex-Met. Railway)
Mid brown, including most ends; roofs usually dull brown of same shade; all frames black. Ends of brake coaches at guard's end, red (not on Ashbury or electric stock). No LT lettering except on driv-

ing cars of T stock. Numbers in gilt at waist level at both ends of sides on all coaches. Destination boards: none on Aylesbury or Chesham trains; ex-Met. Railway black-on-white enamel plates on front and rear of T stock – some later overpainted or fitted with stickers in white on black.

Most Other Electric Stock
As above, but Underground red instead of mid brown. No lettering except on driving coaches, which lower down and not split into two panels; numbers as above but level with lettering. Destination boards white on black.

A Stock
Unpainted aluminium. Letters and numbers as for red stock but originally in Underground red instead of gilt, later bus red (the deeper shade looked almost maroon against the silver).

Open Wagons
Mid grey, black frames below solebars; "LONDON TRANSPORT" in white equal-sized letters, one above the other, at left-hand end; number with initial prefix, usually with full-stops, at right-hand end. Lettering usually hand-painted Johnston, sometimes stencilled and non-Johnston later. Number at each end of sides and legend in centre on flat wagons.

Goods Brake Vans
As above, roofs dull brown, both ends Underground red (bus red after about middle of our period); frames black, lettered as above at one end roughly at waistline; number in centre of available space above waistline on sides and below it on ends. Insides of van dull blue-green, ceiling cream or white, insides of verandas grey.

Small Cranes
As open wagons, lettered where practicable, number usually on frames. Red buffer-beams and liberal touches of red on moving parts; handles and lettering always white.

Small Crane Jib-wagons
As small cranes, numbered but not usually lettered.

Heavy Cranes
Black, single-lined in red (the only use of this livery on LT). Red buffer-beams and many moving parts, white handles; standard gilt legend split into two parts, "LONDON" above "TRANSPORT" on main side panel.

Heavy Crane Jib-wagons
Black, either lined in red or unlined; number in gilt or white at one end or centrally. Examples: lined and lettered, J.683; no lining or lettering, but number in gilt, J.684.

Hopper Wagons
Mid grey; "LONDON TRANSPORT" in equal-sized lettering centrally on body, number on frames, all in white.

Passenger and Goods Vans
The few remaining were mid-grey; roofs brown or grey, "LONDON TRANSPORT" in equal-sized lettering, and number in white where best placed.

Breakdown Vans
Mid grey including ends. Broad black-edged waistband (Underground red, later bus red) bearing gilt numbers at each end of sides and standard gilt legend centrally; roofs brown or grey. Buffer-beams red. Breakdown wagon No. 704 was all grey with the normal black below the solebars and was the only vehicle seen in unrelieved grey with the standard gilt LT logo, except that the letters were equal-sized and not underlined. The number was also gilt.

Electric Passenger Locomotives
Maroon, roofs dull brown. Bufferbeams and solebars bus red. Beading maroon, generally edged with non-metallic gold colour (simpler than pre-war liveries). Standard LT legend across beading below waistline in centre of body. Number at each end of sides, centrally on panel. Large number on each end of body below destination board slots. All numbers in fine gilt, with the appearance of gold leaf. Nameplates centrally on sides, above LT logo, in white metal with black background, in correct Johnston lettering. Met. Railway destination plates (as on T Stock) remained in use for most of locos' lives.

N.B. On at least one locomotive, there was a deterioration in the lining colour used: No. 5 was out-shopped in 1959 lined in a shade nearer steam-loco lemon than the previous gold colour.

Electric Service Locomotives
Maroon, dull brown roofs, black frames. No lining. Standard gilt logo centrally on sides with gilt number at each end of sides.

N.B. Ex-Metropolitan loco No. 9 was not restored to passenger service and was finished as above. Solebars and buffer-beams black, numbers small, no nameplates. Standard LT legend still on a 'plank' across beading, as all locos had at one time.

Passenger Compartment Interiors (based on coach No. 491):
Ceiling and sides down to upholstery level, and party walls above luggage-racks, white; woodwork below racks greyish-cream; ceiling vents black; doors mid-brown as exteriors, numbered "491A" etc. in standard black-edged gilt characters; seat frames also mid-brown, window-frames, door anti-draught screens, front bar of luggage racks, upholstery-trimming beading all varnished teak. 1″ open ends of alarm-cord tubes red; self-adhesive labels re alarm signal and fire extinguishers (white on red and black on red respectively) affixed nearby.

Guards'/luggage compartments: ceiling white; walls blue-green; doors exterior-brown without numbers; brake handle black.

Unpainted aluminium A stock interiors: ceiling white; general finish light grey with brown-red bulkheads, luggage-racks aluminium.

THE APPEARANCE OF STATIONS

LT Section
Most of the paintwork at Harrow-on-the-Hill was a light emerald green, with a varnished finish to wooden doors. An alternative colour for rebuilt stations was a rather severe olive green, as at Eastcote. The standard scheme for older stations comprised a dark brown for canopies, doors and most of the other surfaces including the lower half of pillars, the upper halves of which were pale green, and a cream for under-canopy woodwork and part of the window frames. At mainly wooden stations like North Harrow and Moor Park creosote was the principal finish. LT began experimenting with modern colours in the fifties, when greys were introduced alongside the traditional colours. Sometimes the results were unfortunate, as at Baker Street where the upper halves of pillars were dark grey and the lower parts dark brown of equal tone! Gradually some pleasing schemes were evolved using shades of buff, pale grey, and various blues.

North of Great Missenden

In 1948 almost all the LNER-maintained stations at Great Missenden and north thereof were still finished in the wartime grey which had a greenish-bluish tinge. It was hardly relieved except for a little stone colour, white bands on pillars to show up in the blackout, and a few old blue enamel signs which gave a little sparkle. This scheme could be seen as far north as Verney Junction goods yard (though not at the passenger station which was still in LMS tan and cream) with the exception of Aylesbury. The latter station did not see the grey scheme at all, as it went straight from pre-war cream and two tones of green (shades of the Great Central) into the post-war combination of cream and olive, with pale green ironwork up under the canopies.

The Great Missenden trio were painted in LT's 'old' colours in 1952, and as window-frames were then in brown overall instead of partly cream, the stations' appearance from the street was very forbidding . These three stations remained under LT for maintenance even after the LMR take-over of services in 1961. Great Missenden and Wendover were then finished in a non-standard scheme of mainly cream, grey and a bilious greengage, whereas Stoke Mandeville alone had a pleasing scheme where dark blue replaced the green.

Aylesbury, Quainton Road and Verney Junction were repainted from 1951 onwards in LMR gulf red (a red-brown) and stone. Only Aylesbury of these three survived in passenger service long enough to see a new scheme where black, white and dark blue were the main colours.

PASSENGER STATION PUBLICITY

The line's only example of a fully LT-ised station, Harrow-on-the-Hill, had a very pleasing frontage at both its entrances. Above the standard canopy with the station name in white on blue glass, flanked by "METROPOLITAN LINE & LNER", there appeared in a large glass window the LT symbol and the LNER's 'eye' logo. During the Met. Line modernisation the 'eye' was removed, and a BR totem took its place, which surprisingly was in blue rather than in LMR dark red. It was in due course replaced by the British Rail 'barbed wire' logo in vermilion (more orange than the LT red).

Most of the stations on the line still had the appearance of country stations, and were practically anonymous when seen from the street outside. Some on the LT section which were rebuilt as part of the modernisation acquired standard LT displays – illuminated ring and bar and canopy with blue glass. Those which retained their traditional appearance gradually received modest illuminated boxes under the front canopy above the door, again with the station name on blue glass. Of the stations north of Amersham again under main line control since 1961, Great Missenden stayed anonymous until after BR's 'maroon' period. Wendover and Stoke Mandeville displayed their new ownership by means of maroon enamel signs fitted above a set of poster-boards erected at the station approaches.

Aylesbury station's exterior was unnamed until the provision of maroon enamel signs in 1961, when very large signs were fitted to the canopy. Between the end of the war and 1948 a rather fine sign was put up some distance away at the bottom of the town's market square, pointing into the aptly named Great Western Street. A typical LT enamel sign with cream background, it read approximately: "AYLESBURY STATION: GW & LNE RAILWAYS AND METROPOLITAN LINE"; the last two words were in white on a panel of the green which was standard for the Met. Line as well as the District. An arrow pierced a red ring. At the time of the general provision of dark red signs, it was replaced by a less grand "AYLESBURY TOWN STATION" sign with a BR totem. At the top end of the Market Square a fine sign directed traffic to car parks (on traffic blue background) and to Aylesbury Town station (with maroon background). Judging by the style of lettering this sign was a Ministry of Transport sign erected by the local authority.

Quainton Road was anonymous to the end of its passenger existence, if one discounts a standard-lamp with the name "WEST WYCOMBE" painted out! Verney Junction had at one time a large oil lamp fitted in a 'cage' mounted on a post at the station approach. This lamp had the station name in black letters on the clear glass, and was latterly stored in the booking office, it probably had not been in position since nationalisation.

STATION NAMEBOARDS

Station nameboards on the former Met. & GC main line were by no means uniform at the start of the period; only Harrow-on-the-Hill of the LT group, rebuilt prior to the second world war, exhibited standard signs. These were of the familiar ring-and-bar type, the red of the ring being outlined by fine black lines as was normal at the time. The other ex-LPTB stations displayed a mixture of former Metropolitan Railway signs supplemented with paper rings-and-bars where called for. The Met. boards were of three distinct generations – white on dark blue dating from early days; white, shaded black on vermilion, and the white-lettered blue bar across a red diamond, all on a white background. These diamonds were to be seen, for instance, at North Harrow, Northwood Hills, Moor Park (where they had had new Johnston-lettered blue bars fitted), and Rickmansworth. The latter station also displayed the earlier red-background boards. A full set of these could be seen at Northwood, Chorley Wood (although here the boards were still overpainted with wartime grey, upon which a blue-bar paper sticker was pasted), Chalfont and Latimer, and Amersham. The really early blue signs could only be seen at Pinner and Chesham, where a fine example remained. At Chalfont, a blue "JUNCTION FOR CHESHAM" board could be seen along with main name boards in the red-background style. There was also a similarly worded sign painted in correct Johnston on a red ground.

On this LT section south of Amersham, standard ring-and-bar signs similar to those at Harrow-on-the-Hill first made their appearance after nationalisation, mounted on frames of angle-iron. The double names favoured by the Met. Railway (e.g., Amersham and Chesham Bois), lost their second name with a few exceptions, one being Chalfont and Latimer. Even here the new 1948 signs were merely worded "CHALFONT", but they were soon overpasted with paper strips restoring the full title and varnished; these were first noted on 24th. January 1949. These lasted some years like the similarly overpasted ones at Moor Park. The new rings-and-bars here had been delivered lettered "MOOR PARK &" (sic) with "SANDY LODGE" beneath in much smaller letters. The paper amendments had the ampersand deleted and had as the lower line "AND SANDY LODGE", which was more pleasing. The name eventually became plain "MOOR PARK" however, the blue bars remaining much deeper than on signs that had been single-line from the start.

The former LNER stations Great Missenden to Stoke Mandeville inclusive retained their large original blue signs but these were overpainted with grey backgrounds, on which the huge Grotesque characters were faithfully repainted. When LT renovated these stations in 1952 the now-grey signs were withdrawn leaving only the paper LT signs which had been put up even before the LT take-over. They stayed in situ, renewed as necessary until the LMR took charge in 1961, when similar paper signs bearing temporary totems replaced them pending the arrival of permanent enamel.

At Aylesbury the main boards had screwed-on letters probably dating from the rebuilding in 1925. There was also a single, much older-looking running-in board facing north. All these boards had been painted white on black by the LNER. They were never painted BR blue, but went straight into LMR red in 1951. The red of these painted signs was lighter than the shade of the enamel signs, and was nearer to a cherry red; although the LMR colour was officially maroon, the shades used had not the brownish tinge of, for instance, LT locomotives. Aylesbury also boasted rectangular lamp tablets. They were in the white-on-dark blue enamel which the LNER had adopted after the war, but the use on them of perfect LT Johnston typeface instead of LNER Gill Sans was puzzling. Aylesbury's enamel signs suffixed "TOWN" to distinguish it from Aylesbury High Street (still open for goods) came in 1961. Quainton Road was equipped with meagre plywood boards in imitation of those at Aylesbury. They were painted blue (later dark red) on which the name was painted in correct Gill Sans, and they were positioned adjacent to the oil lamps. In LMR days, large painted running-in boards were put up at the platform ends. No totems or other enamel signs – save a poster heading – were ever provided.

Verney Junction, having been signed by the LMS, still had that company's standard signs with black letters on a yellow 'hawkseye' shape, the whole on a white background. They were later replaced by LMR maroon signs, though no totems were ever provided.

Of the other passenger station signs, those indicating "WAY OUT", "WAITING ROOM", "LADIES" and so on were variously suspended from the canopy ironwork, or fixed to the walls of the buildings so as to project at right angles or were fixed to the doors. Some had frames of wood, bronze or aluminium. There were some interesting survivals in 1948. Amersham had a complete set of Met. red, white and black signs, while at Chalfont and Chesham wooden-framed "WAY OUT" signs in white with heavy black lettering could be seen, which type was also in use at North Ealing on the Piccadilly Line. The above were all enamel but at North Harrow, wooden "WAY OUT" boards persisted. Their background was grained or stippled brown and the words were in off-white (probably white under varnish) shaded black. The "W" and "O" were enlarged, and the two words had a single underline. This dipped in two saucer-shapes to avoid touching the large initial letters. This style of presentation could only be seen elsewhere at a few locations such as on platform benches at Baker Street, a door labelled "INSPECTORS" at Moorgate, and another "WAY OUT" sign at Farringdon which was later pasted over with a modern paper design.

In early 1955 frameless double-sided signs closely resembling the BR version began to appear on the LT section; one of the earliest (at Chorley Wood) indicating "TO TRAINS FOR ..." had blue edging to the white enamel, but soon after, as at Chalfont and Latimer, the signs were unedged white with blue lettering, with a red ring-and-bar where appropriate. Blue had replaced black as the standard lettering colour some years after the war. Harrow, and subsequently other stations, also had internally illuminated box-signs, always white on black.

At about the same time the arrow used on the "WAY OUT" signs and the like was 'sharpened' and the 'feathers' reduced from three or more to just two. The arrow 'pierced' a red circle, which had black outlines (not touching the red) in earlier examples as had the small rings-and-bars where used on these signs. Towards the end of our period the arrow changed yet again; it lost its ring and feathers and came to resemble the arrow used on road signs. LT door plates were small, with rounded corners, coloured as for larger signs. Early plates had a brown or red outline, just within a white border. The three stations taken over in 1948 retained their early Met. Railway door-plates and canopy signs, the latter crudely overpainted by the LNER in white on black, until standard LT signs made their appearance in 1952.

Aylesbury's door-plates were LNER cast iron and their black background was changed to match the new maroon running-in signs. Flanged enamel plates with rounded corners later appeared. At Quainton Road, more Met. Railway blue enamel door-plates and hanging signs survived, and escaped the overpainting inflicted south of Aylesbury. They lasted until closure, and a few even beyond. Under the LMS the signs at Verney Junction were of screwed-on letters on wooden boards, painted black. Here too they changed to LMR red after 1948. The very few enamel signs included a standard "BRITISH RAILWAYS" heading-plate on a poster board outside the station, but these were not provided by BR on boards viewed from the platforms. One wooden sign which became well-known to enthusiasts in the fifties and early sixties was fixed on the footbridge; it directed passengers to the platforms for various destinations "AND METROPOLITAN LINE", this phrase still being picked out in white until it was painted out in maroon.

AYLESBURY STATION

Aylesbury Station was larger than most others on the line and had been rebuilt by the LNER soon after grouping. It had four platforms, the westernmost (No. 4) being used by trains from the

Princes Risborough branch; Platforms 2 & 3 took the through traffic and the bay platform, No. 1, was for terminating suburban trains, particularly those of the Metropolitan Line. There were goods yards at each end of the station; the goods shed and office and cattle dock were at the north yard. There was also a coal yard (slightly enlarged when the High Street station coal yard closed in 1963) adjoining the yard at the south end. There were north and south signal boxes, both of GCR origin, and a smaller structure near the platforms which a station official described as 'the old local box'.

The two-road engine-shed – demolished November 1967 – had the appearance of dating from the early days of the line; it bore a "NO ADMITTANCE" cast-iron plate above the doors headed "GREAT WESTERN RAILWAY" and another plate within was 'signed' "INGLIS, SECRETARY".

Despite the generally LNER atmosphere of most of the premises in 1948 there was still evidence of the other partners – and even foreigners! The large water tower at the north end of Platforms 3/4 had already been replaced by a simple column embossed "GNR 141". A column at the London end of Platforms 1/2 was marked "GWR Wolverhampton Works April 1880". GWR-style cross-by-bridge signs, with the words cast in mixed sizes like a text of scripture, could be seen at the platform ends, latterly in LMR paint. GWR influences could also be noted in the bridge carrying the A 418 Oxford Road over the line beyond the north yard; it was almost identical with that at Culham GWR. The corresponding bridge carrying the Stoke Road at the southern end of the south yard was of starkly plain Met. design. The bridges were numbered MR 160 and 157 respectively.

The GCR had provided most signals, cast-iron trackside signs and a goods yard crane marked "GCR C200". When the tracks were extensively simplified following the end of GC through services, at least two 'new' signalling components were embossed "LMS." Only one permanent item of LT origin (as distinct from posters, etc.,) was ever observed, a small painted metal notice on the station wall advising passengers to lock their cycles. It was in black LT lettering on cream, with ring-and-bar in red and blue.

By the end of 1968 the following had gone from the station: the loco-shed and coaling-stage; the North signal box; all water columns; pre-group signals and GWR signs. The south yard was now largely used for DMU stabling. The parcels office had become the ticket-hall and vice versa, but this arrangement did not last for long and the original set-up was restored.

THE AYLESBURY LINE GOODS YARDS

All the stations on the Met. & GC had coal sidings except the passenger-only stations at North Harrow, Northwood Hills and Moor Park. There were also coal sidings at Wembley Park (served by a separate BR service), Neasden station (as distinct from Neasden Depot) and Willesden Green. At Finchley Road, exchange facilities existed with the Midland line, though no service appeared in the 1950 working timetable. Many of the yards had goods sheds, for example Willesden Green, Harrow-on-the-Hill, Pinner, Northwood, Rickmansworth and all stations to Aylesbury except Stoke Mandeville, and at least fourteen of them had a weighbridge and office. All these facilities were gradually taken out of use during the fifties and sixties, until the freight service over the joint line disappeared altogether by the end of our period – except at Aylesbury, where there had existed a siding into the International Alloys factory premises, and new services to a coal concentration depot and an oil depot were begun, the latter by February 1967. These facilities were all on the north side of Aylesbury station. Enlarged weighbridges were installed at Great Missenden and Willesden Green in 1959 and 1962 respectively. Redundant buildings, where not demolished, were given over to other uses; for instance, Rickmansworth goods shed soon displayed a Kunzle Cakes hoarding, and Amersham weighbridge office was taken over by the Evening News. Coal storage areas at some stations such as Chorley Wood, continued to be used by merchants even after the rails had been lifted.

PUBLICITY AT GOODS YARDS

After 1948 a typical British Railways goods yard would announce its ownership and identity by means of a sign at the entrance in the regional colour reading "BRITISH RAILWAYS – (placename) GOODS & COAL DEPOT." No such standardised signing was provided on the Met. & GC line. It is possible that some signs disappeared during the war years, and certainly after 1945 most goods yards were anonymous. However, among the few that were signed some delightful anomalies existed, partly due to their variously LT or LNER ownership. They are described in the following paragraphs.

Willesden Green
This yard boasted a proud sign at the gates declaring "LONDON TRANSPORT (on red white and blue ring-and-bar) GOODS AND COAL DEPOT". It was lettered in black and the whole sign had a warm mid brown outline a short distance from the extreme edge. The gate pillar bore a smaller sign asking drivers to drive slowly and avoid the weighbridge. Across the fanlight of the weighbridge office door was another sign lettered "GOODS OFFICE". Both the last-named signs bore an unlettered ring-and-bar in colour and were in black and white but without the brown outline of the main sign. The latter, by the way, had its angle-iron frame painted station brown or grey according to period, compared with the teak framing of the lesser signs. After the closure of the yard it found its way to Bucks Railway Centre.

Neasden
No main sign was provided here but a corrugated-iron weighbridge-type hut within the entrance had a painted sign "LTE GOODS OFFICE". The letters were in black on a white ground unframed and it lacked a ring-and-bar. Although detached from the wall it remained in the porch until the end of the freight service.

Wembley Park
Was this London Transport's premises that changed ownership most often? Originally Met. Railway, it became LPTB, LNER, BR(E), BR(W), BR(LM) and finally went back to LT as a car-park! At the start of the period under discussion it had a fine large sign in the rich dark blue of the LNER whose initials it displayed with the usual "GOODS AND COAL DEPOT". It was removed in the fifties and not replaced. The weighbridge office bore a standard Met. Railway "4 TONS" plate indicating the maximum load to be borne. It was in the standard white lettering, shaded black, on a vermilion ground like that at Willesden Green, and both were headed "METROPOLITAN RAILWAY" in full. The one at Wembley Park, however, had had its title overpainted with a vermilion panel after the LNER take-over, whose initials were painted on in simplified style. They were believed to be in unshaded white Gill Sans with raised full-stops between the letters. This panel had weathered off by 1961.

Harrow-on-the-Hill
At Harrow was a wooden sign on a single wooden post. In 1948 it was still in faded bus red with the title of the Met. & GC joint Committee above the usual goods and coal depot wordings though the exact details were unrecorded. In the mid-fifties the sign was repainted with the main area white, the frame light grey and the post mid grey overall. The lettering was "BRITISH RAILWAYS GOODS DEPOT" in black, without ring-and-bar of course, although it was executed in correct LT Johnston style. Near the goods office door was a painted sign fixed to the railings saying simply "GOODS OFFICE   ENQUIRIES". Lettering was again black on a white ground, and the half-round beading bordering it was in cream.

Watford Line
This line showed some interesting variety. The goods shed at Watford was fitted with a large enamel sign reading "METRO & LNER GOODS WAREHOUSE" in white, shaded black, on red. At the passenger station entrance another large sign remained from Met. Railway days. The background was white, the words were black and it had the Met. diamond logo in red, white and blue. It read "METRO AND LNE RAILWAYS   ENTRANCE TO WATFORD (on the logo) PASSENGER STATION, GOODS & COAL DEPOT. FREQUENT SERVICES TO LONDON AND ALL PARTS". A similar sign was to be seen at Croxley Green, and when this station was renamed Croxley in 1949, a plate bearing the new name in standard LT lettering was screwed over the bar of the Met. diamond device. Neither of these two old Met. signs lasted long into the fifties; that at Watford was replaced by a simple sign saying "WATFORD STATION" with "METROPOLITAN LINE" on a purplish strip. Thereafter goods were not mentioned. A painted sign in interesting colours was fitted to Croxley goods yard gates, however, which read "NO ADMITTANCE FOR PASSENGERS" (in white on a red background) "GOODS TRAFFIC ONLY" followed by the ring-and-bar. The last three words and sign were in olive green letters on a cream ground.

Chesham
This was the only other goods yard in outer Metroland with an identity sign. It was a wooden board fixed to the goods office wall. At the beginning of the time being described it was lettered "CHESHAM GOODS STATION   ENQUIRIES" but it did not 'let on' who owned it! The words, in nondescript style, were in black on a cream background whose frame was dark brown. During a general repaint of the premises during the fifties the board was repainted overall mid grey. The wording, now in correct Johnston, was "GOODS OFFICE   LONDON MIDLAND REGION   CHESHAM" in white.

Other Signs
The "4 TONS" weighbridge plates referred to earlier were affixed at these yards north of Harrow inclusive: Northwood, Chorley Wood, Chalfont and Latimer, Amersham, Great Missenden and Wendover. They were all the same colours as the two south of Harrow except that the one at Chalfont lacked the black shading to the words. Other signs were not common; some yards on the LT section acquired speed limit signs in white on red; at Aylesbury a few standard maroon signs were put up and there had been few old LNER signs with raised letters. One was headed "LNER", another "AYLESBURY JOINT STATION" or a contraction thereof, and received maroon paint before enamel signs were introduced. A third title seen at this station was "MET. & GC RLY" which was on a large board at the rail-wagon weighbridge instructing engines not to pass over it. It remained in LNER white on black until removal.

Both Chesham and Rickmansworth had an enamel "PRIVATE ROAD" sign near the goods yard. These were lettered in ultramarine on cream and headed "METROPOLITAN AND GREAT CENTRAL JOINT COMMITTEE" in full. This colour scheme was standard for certain purposes and could also be seen on a sign at Hillingdon which read "TRESPASSERS WILL BE PROSECUTED" and bore the ring-and-bar in full colour. A sign at Ruislip warning road traffic to keep clear of the weighbridge had black letters on a white ground and a bronze frame, the post being station brown, and another similar sign had a red frame.

STATION LIGHTING

Needless to say, the stations on the London end of the line were already electrically lit at the start of our period, but we only needed to travel out as far as Chorley Wood to find a platform lit by gas. Gas lamps could also be seen on the down platform at Amersham in the early years. Wendover was largely gas-lit too, and as it remained thus until 1965, new copper gas lamps were installed during

1962 on the recently extended platforms. Moreover, the signal box remained gas-lit as long as it was in use (after 1983). Stoke Mandeville's platforms were oil-lit until 1965, although a gas light illuminated the porch, and there was electricity on the bridge and in the main rooms. Quainton Road's platforms were also oil-lit until closure in 1963, and again there was a minimum of electricity; Verney Junction retained oil lamps until the end.

CLOSED STATIONS

Only two stations once served by trains of the Met. & GC Joint line were closed after 1948: Quainton Road and Verney Junction, although by then there was of course no service between them; only trains on the Oxford and Banbury to Bletchley lines still served Verney Junction. Quainton Road was served in 1948 by about seven passenger trains in each direction. The goods yard was busy; it had a weighbridge but no goods shed. A notice detailing hours of business for goods was affixed to the wall of the passenger station. The line from Quainton Road to Verney Junction had already been singled by the time of nationalisation although it still ran right through to Verney Junction and was signalled at both ends. The goods yard at the latter station remained, complete with signal box and signalling, all apparently out of use. At this time it was clear that Verney Junction had been under shared ownership; the ex-LMS passenger station was still in brown and cream and the tracks were signalled by modern upper quadrants, while the Met. & GC yard buildings and posts still languished under their coat of wartime grey. The signals here were almost all of GC pattern, though at least one LNER standard disc signal was in place. The box was closed and had no nameboard; some of the signals were permanently in the 'off' position. After 1948 two small but standard LMR dark red enamel name boards were put up, but no totems were ever used. The ticket hall at the station entrance was disused, and tickets were issued from a window on the platform. The station did not alter greatly during our twenty years. I was told that bridges were becoming unsafe by the summer of 1956 and all the buildings in the Met. & GC yard were demolished, the signalling removed and the tracks simplified into sidings for the storage of old coaching stock. The former main line was redoubled as far as Winslow Road but was lifted between that former station and Quainton Road. Rail-chairs on the former Met. main line had been variously marked MS&L RLY 1892, MR 1901/2/3, MET. & GC 1910 and LMS. The existing buffer-stop at Winslow Road was of GC/LNER 3-rail type, and was joined by a 2-rail LMR type on the new siding. What must surely have been the last passenger train to venture from Verney Junction as far as Winslow Road was the enterprising "Chiltern 200" tour organised by the Railway Enthusiasts' Club in 1963. Verney Junction passenger station closed on the first day of 1968, and everything except the platforms was demolished by October. According to a press report, goods facilities there had been withdrawn during January 1964, though it is difficult to see what services could still have been offered; no doubt the odd wagon could have been dealt with on the storage sidings!

Immediately on closure the name "Verney Junction" was dropped from the replacement bus timetables, in favour of "East Claydon, Verney Arms". The traditional name may he seen today however on DoE road signs, on ordnance maps and in the 'phone-book, and seems to have survived the bus company's attempts to suppress it. Another example of a former Met. & GC station name persisting (though strictly outside the scope of this book) is that of Wood Siding on the Brill branch. This name – often spelt as one word – could be seen in bus timetables some forty years after closure, and is even more remarkable as not even a hamlet exists at this location, just a single house some distance away. Even in the 90's the name was still used to describe this lonely spot in some local publications.

In 1948 Quainton Road's buildings, signals and other paintwork were still in the wartime grey. The only name boards were as described in the appropriate chapter. Early Met. blue enamel signs still hung from the canopy and appeared on doors. The few signals were of GC or LNER upper quadrant type and there were ground discs of standard LNER design. Poster-boards on the station walls were headed by LNER blue enamel plates, except that where "LONDON TRANSPORT" or "LNER & LT" headings were called for they were hand-painted on to strips of steel. Soon after nationalisation such plates referring to LT were removed, exposing the previous pillar-box red ground from which the earlier "METROPOLITAN" letters had been unscrewed. As these had originally been fixed on to a black ground, the word was plainly legible: thus the boards once again read "LNER" and "METROPOLITAN" instead of "LNER" and "LT". Although the LNER plates were equally obsolete, it was some time before they were removed and the boards painted plain black. A few electric lights were in use in key positions – booking office, over the footbridge – but most of the lighting was provided by oil lamps mainly of the standard design used on the Met. At the front of each lamp was a panel bearing the station name, either in ultramarine lettering on uncoloured glass, or on uncoloured frosted glass where the background only was filled in with black forming a stencil. During the twenty years, the station was repainted a few times in LMR gulf red and cream.

After the station closed in 1963, a bulk car traffic began from the yard to Bathgate, Scottish Region, but this only lasted from February until September 1965. Even before final closure to freight traffic in 1966, the local authorities were giving their approval to use of the site by the London Railway Preservation Society.

SIGNAL BOXES

At the start of the period, most of the signal boxes on the Met. and GC line were of Met. Railway origin. Exceptions were Harrow-on-the-Hill where the box was incorporated in the station buildings, and Aylesbury North and South which were of GC origin. A new brick box was built at the north end of Rickmansworth down platform before the Met. modernisation, and a new box of composite metal and brick construction was put up at Amersham. Traditional boxes were gradually reduced in number, that at Watford South Junction being one of the earliest to go, and others went during the modernisation; some were replaced by windowless brick structures (e.g. Chorley Wood, 1954). Some of the surviving boxes were put to different uses.

In Met. Railway days many boxes were provided with a large nameboard fixed beneath the windows on the front. Each was a plain wooden plank with semi-circular ends. These boards survived on the main line at Northwood, Watford South Junction, Chorley Wood, Chalfont and Latimer and Amersham. On the ex-LNER section these boards had long been replaced by those of LNER style with screwed on metal letters. A board was fixed just below the eaves at each end of the box, and this arrangement could be seen at all stations from Great Missenden northward, including the two GC boxes at Aylesbury, but there were no boards on the box at Verney Junction in 1948.

In the late forties boxes on the LT section were usually finished in cream with dark brown frames, banisters, handrails etc. giving a pleasant half-timbered house effect. At their last repaint in this scheme in 1951, the boxes from Watford South Junction to Amersham inclusive had their name boards removed for repainting. They were beautifully refinished in gloss white with the name executed in black in perfect Johnston. Thereafter, when LT dabbled in modern colours some boxes were finished in grey and cream in varying proportions, with white, cream or grey boards lettered in black or even red. Chorley Wood's board was noteworthy in that it was repainted cream during a fifties box-repaint in grey and cream with huge 'old fashioned' expanded lettering. It was also believed to be the last survivor of these hand-painted Met. boards still to be lettered. The new brick structures and a few of the traditional boxes (e.g., Chesham) received new enamel nameplates, blue on white, still in the traditional Met. position on the front. That at Amersham was worded "SIGNAL BOX JW". Similar buildings with other uses received the same type of plate, for example "INTER-LOCKING MACHINE ROOM JD" at Northwood.

Boxes formerly under LNER control were still in all-over wartime grey in 1948, except the two boxes at Aylesbury which had been finished post-war in LNER olivish-green and cream with black boards. Boxes taken over by LT in 1948 were finished in all over dark brown with cream window-frames at first though by 1963 grey was replacing the brown. At Aylesbury and Quainton Road boxes were refinished in LMR gulf red (red oxide) soon after nationalisation, and in 1965 dull olive and stone were applied to the former box. The box at Verney Junction retained the faded war-grey until demolished.

Nameboards on the now LMR boxes at Aylesbury and Quainton Road were correctly finished in 1951 in regional dark red with white letters. LNER boxes taken over by LT continued to have their boards painted in white on black in LNER fashion, which style persisted after 1968 – in fact until the boxes were taken out of use or demolished. None of the boards at these three stations was ever finished in the correct BR maroon. After 1961 Stoke Mandeville boards were unique in their treatment. They received dark brown backgrounds of the same hue as the body of the box, and in 1964 both box and boards were repainted light grey. Lettering was always white.

SIGNALS

On the half of the Met. & GC that had always been under Met. control the signals where they had not been replaced by colour lights were still of the standard design used by the Met. Railway (which could also be seen on ex-LBSCR lines). The wooden posts had flattened pointed iron caps compared with the ball-and-spike finials of GC signals, though the arms were rather similar apart from the rounded corners of the GC type. The semaphore nearest to London (which somehow had acquired a perforated-ball and spike finial) was No. G17 in Pinner goods yard; another rather fine signal stood by Northwood signal box; its three 'dolls' were numbered E8, E13 and E16. Dwarf signals had originally been miniature semaphores, but all except those at Chesham had been provided years ago with enamelled discs similar to BR standard discs but much larger. They had the usual red and blue-green glasses except one in Rickmansworth goods yard which had red and amber only and was normally in the 'off' position. Late replacements by LT still had a rudimentary post and central spindle, though the discs were floodlit. On the final type of standard disc installed at the time of the Met. modernisation the central boss was absent . The Met. section had a remarkable survivor: it was a small yellow distant arm fitted to the post of Rickmansworth's down starter though facing north; it was to repeat the indication of the up starter, not easily visible to trains approaching from the Chorley Wood direction due to the curvature of the track. This arm was of the early balanced design with circular glasses, though no stub-arm was fitted to the spectacle-plate. At the time of the Met. Line modernisation some remarkable temporary signals appeared on the line: one was the up distant at Chalfont, which seemed to utilise a former trolleybus wire-supporting post from the roadside; the arm was pivoted almost centrally, so that in the off position it almost disappeared against the ample girth of the post. Another temporary signal was Amersham's up starter, which had a fluted enamel arm on a tubular post of normal width. The arms of these signals could have been re-used arms from District Line semaphores which had been taken down a few years earlier; a disused spectacle-plate from one of these was seen near Chalfont box at the time the temporary signals went up. These fittings were enamelled and had round spectacles; a characteristic was that they were mostly red except for the surround to the green glass which was white.

On the ex-GC section from Great Missenden to Verney Junction inclusive most signals were of GC design on wooden posts. Some posts had been replaced by concrete ones as far back as 1918. Replacement arms could be identified by their having sharp ends to the blades compared with the rounded corners of the original GC arms. Upper quadrant arms had appeared pre-second world war; the down distant at Stoke Mandeville was dated 1938, and several lower quadrant arms were replaced in the Aylesbury area not long afterwards. Disc signals were almost universally of GC style until the mid-war years. Each had a white recessed centre to the red disc, and the whole signal rotated at right angles to display a green aspect. Mostly they were replaced by LNER disc signals which had a red horizontal stripe; the disc rotated in the vertical plane to display the stripe diagonally – and a green light – to indicate 'line clear'. Some of these signals were replaced in turn by a BR standard type which was not dissimilar. The discs of this type were not quite vertical but tipped slightly backwards at the top; they thus faced more squarely towards a driver's viewpoint and could be arranged in banks with two or more signals on top of each other without any disc fouling an adjacent one. One of the GC recessed centre signals survived at Stoke Mandeville until signalling there was abolished in 1966. There were a few Met. Railway dwarf signals of varying styles as well in Stoke Mandeville goods yard, but these appeared second-hand after the LT take-over and did not date from Met. days.

Two more really ancient Metropolitan survivals could still be seen on the line at the start of our period. One was a three-arm semaphore signal in Verney Junction goods yard. It was of the early Met. Railway type with circular glasses to the spectacle-plate behind which extended stub-arms to balance the main blade and ensure a return to danger. This signal lingered on until the box and all Met. & GC signals were abolished in 1957, by which time two of the arms on the three-arm signal had lost their extension blades. All other signals withdrawn at that time were of GC origin, and all posts were still painted wartime grey with only short black bases. Signalling remaining on the running lines through the station was all of LMS/BR design.

The other survivor from Met. Railway days controlled backing into the refuge from the up platform at Wendover. It seemed to be a Great Centralised Met. type, a ball-and-spike finial having at sometime been added. It retained the round-spectacle-plate (without 'tail' blade, though marks on the rear showed where it had once been fixed), a large 'dish' where a big Met. lamp had been fitted, and an octagonal weight on the lever. During the paintless war years, LNER paint had worn off, revealing original Met. Railway vermilion with a black stripe as used on subsidiary signals in earlier times. It regained its white stripe after the war. It remained in position, well-buttressed by lengths of bullhead rail, until signalling at Wendover was withdrawn in 1966.

LINESIDE SIGNS

Where public rights of way crossed the line it was usual for a pair of cast iron signs to be provided at each side, one of each pair telling users to beware of the trains, and the other warning of penalties for trespass from the line of the right-of-way. On the Met. Railway part of the line the "BEWARE" signs had rounded corners and were headed "MET RLY". "NO TRESPASSING" signs were often of a GC type which announced a penalty of 40 shilling (sic). This particular sign was one of the few to be found on both sides of the Met./main line boundary at Gt. Missenden. There were other Met. Railway anti-trespass signs with rounded corners, and a sharp-cornered style warning of the danger of conductor rails. Most of these were anonymous, but a very rare version gave the company's title in full; one was to be seen at Northwood.

Some old catch points signs, with the top edge rising into a 'gable' could be seen around Amersham. These usually had "CATCH POINT" (in the singular) in screwed-on letters. Elsewhere on the Harrow-Amersham section the standard LT catch points signs with black Johnston lettering on white became almost universal. Their frames were at one time varnished, but red became the norm. Only one double-sided sign of this type appeared on LT's newly acquired Great Missenden to Aylesbury line, just south of the first-named station. Its frames were painted white. Standard LT signs of any sort remained few on this section. Another enamel sign used by LT was the "STOP" board. It was of shallow diamond shape, lettered in white on a vermilion ground. There were some in Harrow goods yard and one at Rickmansworth. Their frames were often red or silver, though they could be seen painted black.

During the sixties some neat enamel signs, not very tall, were put in on the electrified lines and indicated where points were heated in winter months. The 'flags' were oblong, frameless, flanged and with rounded corners, and were lettered in white on bus red.

Another series – or strictly two series – of signs were provided along the permanent way of the LT lines. Looking like miniature gradient posts, their stubby arms bore two numbers, e.g. 20-21 near Amersham, 21-22 north of Great Missenden, and 22-BR which stood at the down side of the line where LT maintenance ended half way between Stoke Mandeville and Aylesbury. On the up side was a triangular-section post put in by BR with "NORTHAMPTON DIVISION LMR/LONDON TRANSPORT EXECUTIVE" on the appropriate faces, but this wooden post soon rotted. The posts of the other series on the LT section referred to above also had short concrete arms and were interspersed among the first series. They bore higher numbers, for example 155-158 near Amersham and 161-170 which was centrally fitted to milepost 28½, the old LT/LNER boundary. The highest numbered post in this series was 172-173.

On the ex-LNER part of the line warning and trespass signs were of GC origin of two distinct styles. The larger was a perfect oblong, whereas the smaller had incurved corners. The former had 'chunky' lettering contrasting with the 'spidery' words on the latter. Usually the "BEWARE" signs were of the first-named type and the smaller warned against trespass. At the top of each sign would be some form of the joint committee's title. Near Stoke Mandeville could be seen a set of the small incurved signs with chunky lettering, but this was an exception. An oddity was the provision of a full set of four signs (two beware, two trespass) headed "MET. & GC RAILWAY" or a variant thereof, at a foot-crossing on the 'pure' GC line nearly a mile from Met. & GC territory north of Quainton Road!

Where catch points were provided on the GC/LNER section they were usually of LNER standard type with two boards at right angles so as to be visible from each direction. They had large screwed-on letters and were on concrete posts. There were a few much older-looking signs with an odd mixture of serif and sans lettering; two of these were to be seen north and south of Stoke Mandeville. Another non-standard catch point sign could be seen near Quainton Road. It was of the 'gable' variety as seen at Amersham, but lacked raised letters. The sign was therefore hand-lettered in near-Gill Sans.

"WHISTLE" signs were not common on the line before 1968. At Rickmansworth a small one was provided on the north approach which had white letters on a beaded wooden board painted red. At the opposite end of the sharp station curve was another sign, a frameless wooden board lettered black on a white ground in a nondescript style. Later the board, together with the lamp casing and post, were finished in overall silver, correctly lettered in black Johnston – the only sign I ever saw in this combination of colours. A very large "WHISTLE" sign could be seen on the southern approach to Aylesbury. It had screwed-on letters, and was probably of LNER origin. It was one of the very few signs that received an ER blue background during the 1948-1950 period, but spent most of its time with a black background.

On the LT-maintained section, cast iron signs were nearly always black on white (with rare periods when the colours were reversed) whereas on BR they were almost always white on black irrespective of LNER, ER or LMR ownership. Exceptions were a very few signs at Aylesbury station, which were painted blue or (later) maroon.

BRIDGE PLATES

Bridges on the Met. main line, which included humbler structures such as culverts – were numbered from MR 1 at the Baker Street tunnels to MR 198 at the last road-bridge before Verney Junction. Most had received in early years the standard Met. Railway bridge number-plate of oblong design with incurved corners. These bore the number in seriffed figures with the letters MR above in a sans-serif style. They were almost always black and white; the LNER painted them white on black, the LMR the opposite, while LT varied between the two.

Over the years some plates had been replaced by more modern designs on the LT-maintained sections. These had radiused corners and the letters preceded the numerals, which were sometimes in a nondescript style (e.g. MR 66 near Pinner) or in almost correct Johnston like MR 44 at Harrow and MR 121 near Great Missenden. There were other completely non-standard ones such as 104 near Chalfont with metal figures screwed onto a square board without initials. Replacements on the former LNER section were rare, but those that did appear were of the oval LNWR type and were affixed in BR days; for some reason none of this type were seen south of Aylesbury. One non-standard type dating from early years was to be seen on the road-bridge at Quainton Road, and was a plain oblong of sheet metal upon which the number A 184 was rather crudely painted. Renumbered BR 184, the new plate disappeared soon after. Other missing plates were not replaced but the number, without initials, was painted directly on to the brickwork, sometimes with a white oblong background. As with the oval plates, these plateless numbers were never seen south of Aylesbury.

During 1963 a new design of plate appeared on the LT section of line. These new plates were again oblong with rounded corners, of greater length than the earlier ones. They bore, from left to right, the initials MR (a happy perpetuation of the old company initials) followed by the number in larger characters, all in correct Johnston style. The characters all had a common base-line. The plates were turned out with glorious abandon, some bridges ending up with one old Met. plate and two of the new type. As LT were still in charge of the former Metropolitan line as far as Aylesbury South Junction at the time the new plates were fitted, they appeared as far north as a culvert just inside the LT/LMR boundary near Stoke Mandeville Hospital which was numbered MR 154.

Initially the new plates were finished in white on black, with the frames not picked out. Later repaints of some plates did have this refinement. Their finish seemed to affect the painting of the older plates too, as many earlier ones were painted white on black from this time onward, with the frames almost always picked out. A few older plates on the LT maintained section had the letters MR on a separate small plate bolted over the original initials, as if LT at one time contemplated introducing initials to suit the joint line but thought better of it, and some MR plates on the Chesham branch acquired small "C" plates as a prefix to the existing initials. Other middle-aged plates incorporated the CMR from the outset, as did those of the latest design in the 60's.

MILEPOSTS

The mileage of the Met. main line was measured from Baker Street towards Verney Junction. The standard Met. Railway milepost had a wooden head of triangular section mounted on a post of bullhead rail, and could be seen as far northwards as Milepost 38 just south of Aylesbury South signal box. Northwards of this point most posts were of LNER type with iron heads on posts of concrete. Early ordnance maps show mileage measured from Verney Junction towards Aylesbury on the Aylesbury & Buckingham section, and the fact that the Met. style of post did not appear north of Aylesbury suggests that the A&BR had already its own posts, all of which had disappeared long before our period. Between the old division of maintenance at MP 28½ and Aylesbury, the standard triangular-headed posts only marked the complete miles; the intermediate fractions were indicated by LNER standard posts. South of Great Missenden, fractional posts as well as those showing complete miles were of the Met. standard type, and at some stage had received screwed-on figures. On the Great Central main line the track was measured from Manchester, the sequence stopping at Quainton Road Junction (where the LMR installed a post giving detailed measurements – see illustration) and starting again south of Harrow. Towards the end of our period all posts on BR territory were painted chrome yellow with black characters. The LT posts, i.e. from MP 25 north of Amersham to a point just south of Harrow, remained black on white. At least one of the LNER posts numbered in the GC series just on the London side of Harrow – No 197 – remained in LT white; the thought of LT owning a milepost showing nearly 200 miles from Manchester is interesting!

GRADIENT POSTS

The earliest gradient posts on the former joint line appear to have been a Met. design with rounded wooden arms on a wooden post. As with mileposts, the posts south of Great Missenden had received screwed-on letters in earlier years, leaving examples at that station and north thereof to be signwritten. Between Amersham and Great Missenden, a few early examples of a non-standard concrete design could be seen.

On the ex-GC/LNER territory many replacements had been provided of LNER style. These had large square-ended wooden arms with very legible screwed-on letters, all on a concrete post. Many standard BR-type concrete posts were put in as replacements at the time of the Met. Line modernisation, particularly between Harrow and Aylesbury. The few remaining hand-lettered posts on the ex-LNE section were extremely long-lived, the last (at Stoke Mandeville) surviving until the nineties; it is now in the museum at Bucks Railway Centre.

BUFFER STOPS

On the ex-Met. sections of the line the oldest buffer-stops had a wooden beam, often with semicircular ends. LT-built stops often had a 'beam' composed of three lengths of bullhead rail laid horizontally. LNER stops also had three lengths of bullhead, but arranged vertically, i.e., with the sides facing the traffic. Some LMR replacements were put in – for instance at Verney Junction – which had only two pieces of rail, left unpainted. Most buffer-stops had a black frame irrespective of ownership, but whereas the LNER painted their 'beams' white (as did succeeding owners with experiments at Aylesbury in yellow), LT beams were almost always red, with the ends neatly painted white. Where 'over riders' were fitted, these were usually painted white too.

OLD "GROUNDED" COACH BODIES

Old coach bodies, removed from their wheels so as to be used as huts, etc., were not common on on the line; in fact only two are known, one at Harrow-on-the-Hill goods yard and one at Aylesbury. Part of a third, possibly of MSLR or GCR build, could be seen on a smallholding near Aylesbury North signal box and while it may have been on railway property it was no longer in railway use. It was later inspected with a view to preservation but was beyond repair.

The body at Harrow, also apparently of MSLR-GCR origin, was in a mid brown livery and was lettered "C & W EXAMINERS No 257" in lemon. It bore no signs of ownership, in fact the only lettering was a metal "A" screwed on to each solebar. The interior was equipped with pigeon-holes containing various wagon-spares and a table of office equipment, the whole being lit by electric light. The body at Aylesbury was from Met. Railway carriage No. 212. The exterior had long been finished in the station colours of the time, so latterly it was in LMR cream with gulf red on the three doors still in use. It stood behind the locoshed, and when one of the shed roads needed to be extended through the back of the shed, the old body was moved some ten feet sideways in 1955. By 1967 it was the property of the BR Sports and Social Association, and was earmarked for use as a pavilion on the nearby sports field (long known as the Oval). However this plan did not come to fruition and the body was burnt the same year – but not before the author had cadged a door for preservation. During stripping, an original class numeral "3" was uncovered, but was not complete enough for retention. Every nail used in the construction of the door was copper, and every screw was brass, so most were used in the rebuilding. This body too was electrically lit. The Harrow body suffered the same fate some years later.

A FEW STATION AND LINESIDE FEATURES

Platform Benches

A design with two wooden backrest bars and seat all carried on three iron supports was in almost universal use from Harrow-on-the-Hill to Quainton Road, with the exception of Aylesbury. Under the Met. Railway they had had the station-name painted on the top bar on a panel of colour with semi-circular ends. This treatment persisted at Watford until as late as 1951. The panel was bright red with white lettering, probably shaded in black.

On the formerly GCR/LNER-maintained section the benches had acquired the station-names in screwed-on letters many years ago in place of the painted word(s). The benches on LT's newly-acquired Great Missenden-Stoke Mandeville line had the letters chiselled off during their first renovation by LT in 1952, but those at Quainton Road remained in place until after closure. The latter station's benches were painted gulf red throughout our period after the wartime grey had been superseded. Benches at Great Missenden-Stoke Mandeville were station brown for about 10 years and then black. Those on the rest of the LT section, including the named Watford ones, were brown initially but were later finished in one of the more modern station colours – dark red, blue or grey. At the time of the Met. modernisation the existing benches were supplemented by new all-teak benches of plain design with vertically-slatted backs. All-wooden designs also persisted in station waiting-rooms from an earlier period. By 1967, new benches were appearing north of Great Missenden too, a very stout design in wood and metal.

Porters' Barrows and Luggage Trolleys

These were latterly supplied by the LMR even to some LT stations, and were sprayed in a mid brown. A typical example inspected at Amersham had an inconspicuous number in small metal characters with 'M' prefix or suffix, though it was clearly lettered "AMERSHAM LTE" in white.

Speed Restriction Signs

LT showed speed restrictions by means of circular enamel plates approximately two feet in diameter. They had the maximum speed – no initials – in black on a white ground within a black border. On the ex-GC/LNER section the few signs were in cut-out numbers on metal posts, the figures being at first white and later yellow.

Water Columns and Towers

Water columns and towers on the LT section were usually in station brown in 1948 (e.g. the tower at Finchley Road). The one at Harrow goods yard ended its LT service with the tank in bridge grey (a light blue-greenish shade) and the column black. Tank-less columns at Great Missenden were mid grey in the sixties after the universal brown fell from favour.

Aylesbury's three columns on the platforms remained in the LNER's 1946 olive green until they were demolished in July 1965; that at the engine shed similarly stayed in its 1946 LNER mid brown. The latter three columns bore three white stripes about 9″ wide around them, separated by two stripes of the background colour. The ex-GNR column at the north end of the station bore one stripe only which was about 6″ wide.

Bridge Paintwork

Bridges were constructed in various materials – steel, concrete, brick (of which yellow London stocks were typical, as in many ex-Metropolitan Railway buildings) – and the paintwork on the LT section in the early years of our survey was almost universally brown similar to the 'old station' colour, named as "Natal Brown" on the paint-cans used. During the sixties a new shade as mentioned in the paragraphs on water columns was introduced. It was a light turquoise-grey and was said to have been voted for by the public as rendering bridges as inconspicuous as possible against the average sky. It was applied to steelwork and woodwork alike, even to the porches at the foot of some staircases and under-stairs cupboard doors, where station colours would have looked more appropriate. Some of the bridge steelwork on the ex-LNER section was painted very dark brown in LMR days.

Loading Gauges

These were finished in the current scheme of the rest of the premises. Stoke Mandeville's was in station brown in 1952 and that at Willesden Green was all over pure light grey in the years before closure of the yard.

Station Poster-boards

Throughout the period London Transport had a standard style for poster-boards both outside stations and those viewed from the platforms. They had no heading-plates indicating ownership, but were plain boards painted mainly grey. The outer beading was white, within which was a border of black about 3" wide, of which a small amount showed when posters were affixed. The ex-LNER boards on the Great Missenden-Stoke Mandeville line bore that company's blue enamel plates lettered "LNER", "LONDON TRANSPORT" or some combination of the two, which LT removed at the 1952 renovation. Many of the plates served as lawn-edging in a retired railwayman's garden for the next 30 years! The tops of the boards that had held the plates were sawn off and the boards repainted to conform with the white, black and grey scheme. This finish was only used on boards displaying timetables and other railway posters; the few boards for purely commercial use could be plain black or another colour. At some LMR stations large boards were provided which carried several small posters. Each poster-space was beaded in black, likewise the outer beading to the whole board; the intervening surround was painted dark red.

At the BR stations heading plates were removed from platform boards but they were otherwise unaltered, merely being painted black overall. Outside stations boards were also all black but were fitted with new dark red "BRITISH RAILWAYS" plates in place of the blue LNER variety.

Platelayers' Huts

There were plenty of the traditional sleeper-built platelayers huts, tarred without and whitewashed within, on the line; they could be seen both sides of the LT/LNER divide at Great Missenden. Others of modern concrete construction were erected by LT after 1948. They appeared to be of Southern design, even to the grass-green paintwork. The outermost was at the end of Stoke Mandeville platform, though this was later replaced by a 'garden shed'. The LNER had also put in a few modern concrete examples; one could be seen near MP 36½ on the way to Aylesbury, and there was at least one south of Harrow on the BR section.

A privately-owned parcels lorry at Wendover on 15th. April 1966. The same firm's board also appeared in the coal yard at Stoke Mandeville.

HARROW-ON-THE-HILL TO VERNEY JUNCTION

PHOTOGRAPHS

Wendover Station, 8th. March 1964.

The most famous of them all, Class A3 Pacific No. 60103 "Flying Scotsman", was used on the GC line for a spell. Here it waits to depart northwards from Aylesbury on 28th. April 1952. The water-crane is marked "GNR 141".

The "Royal Scot" was another type that was used on Marylebone expresses during the last years of steam. Here a dirty 46156 awaits the right-away at Aylesbury on 20th. December 1963.

A none-too-clean "Britannia" No. 70054 is seen at Aylesbury on a typical Nottingham – Marylebone train on 2nd. October 1965.

It was normal for certain Nottingham – Marylebone trains to be double-headed when this picture was taken at Aylesbury on 31st. December 1964. Here unlined 'Black Five' No. 45215 heads No. 45190.

Fast run! 'Black Five' No. 45065 runs into Harrow with the 4.55 p.m. arrival from Marylebone to Nottingham on a day in 1965. The station clock shows about 4.51. No provision was made to show these steam trains on the fairly new indicators.

'Black Five' No. 44835 on a typical evening express from Nottingham to Marylebone calls at Aylesbury on 12th. December 1964. A DMU occupies the bay previously used by the Met. Line trains.

43

Although this picture of LT ex-Met. Class E 0-4-4T No. L.46 on a Baker Street train at Aylesbury was taken on 24th. July 1946, an identical scene could have been recorded on many occasions up to the early fifties.

Tender-first B1 power for a Met. Line train at Aylesbury during 1951, the loco being 61164. The LNER nameboard-boxes with their Johnston lettering may be seen on the lamp-posts.

At Aylesbury: BR Standard Class 4 2-6-0 No. 76044 unusually heads an evening train to Baker Street during 1955.

A typical Met. Line train of six Dreadnoughts hauled by LMS-designed Class 4 2-6-4T No. 42082 at Stoke Mandeville on 16th. August 1960. The platforms had recently been extended to accommodate the longer diesel trains soon to be introduced.

Ample tender-first power for a Met. train to Baker Street: Standard Class 5 4-6-0 No. 73010. Aylesbury, 17th. August 1960.

Despite nationalisation, the successors to the old companies still kept to their traditional haunts at Aylesbury GW & GC and Met. & GC joint station. Here is a very rare shot of a Met. Line train parked on ex-GW & GC territory south of Aylesbury South signal box on 30th. March 1959. The nearest coach, No. 443, is a quarter of a mile towards Princes Risborough! Note the GC sign lettered "GW & GC …" in white on black.

Bedecked with bunting and crew (Fireman Jim Reading and Driver Ken Langston), 0-4-2T No. 1440 waits at Aylesbury Town during the last day of push-and-pull working on the former GW & GC Princes Risborough branch. The loco is still plain black with the old totem. 17th. June 1962.

Class 2 2-6-2T No. 41270 struggles to haul eight coaches packed with football fans bound for High Wycombe up the bank from Aylesbury towards South Aylesbury halt on 30th March. 1959. Note the express passenger headlamps!

This improvised train, using one of the Chesham shuttle sets and one of the regular Chesham engines, was one of the few trains to run locally during the 1955 ASLEF strike. Here it is on arrival at Rickmansworth on about 14th. June 1955.

The Met. electric locos were not often photographed hauling Ashbury coaches, but here is No.2 effecting the Chesham shuttle changeover at Rickmansworth on 21st. August 1960, a few weeks before electric services to Chesham began. The train will terminate at Wembley Park then head for Neasden Depot. It had loaded with parcels, including watercress traffic, and, surprisingly for an early Sunday morning train, is carrying about 60 passengers.

The Chalfont shuttle, still in grained finish, waits at Chesham on 22nd. May 1955. The signal arm shows a small white light instead of red when at danger.

At Chalfont: double-ended power for the Chesham shuttle on 20th. August 1957; sometimes a passenger van or even a GC coach was used in place of the van.

T stock has temporarily taken over the Chesham shuttle on the first day of electric operation, 12th. September 1960, and is here seen at Chalfont and Latimer. The coaches are 2735, 9800 and 2737.

Ex-Met. Railway electric locomotive No. 4, Lord Byron, then nameless in its wartime grey livery, waits at Baker Street with the 5.08 p.m. to Quainton Road on 30th. August 1947. The grey was relieved by Underground red window-frames, backgrounds to end numbers (only) and to LT logos, and beading between roof and body. The logos were in standard black-edged gilt, the numbers in black-edged non-metallic gold colour. The end number-panels had an unedged outline in the same colour.

LNER ex-GCR Class A5 4-6-2T No. 9821 arrives at Quainton Road Met. & GC with a Met. Line train from Liverpool Street on 30th. July 1947. The engine is plain black with red-shaded yellow letters and numbers.

Despite appearances this is the 5.20 p.m. LMR train from Aylesbury to Calvert calling at Quainton Road one day in 1962. The push-and-pull coach was otherwise in use on the Princes Risborough line, having replaced two ordinary coaches when Little Kimble became unstaffed. A local goods engine was sometimes used on the Calvert service – even a WD 90XXX on one occasion – though here No. 1453 provides more matching motive power.

There is time for a chat before the guard presses the buzzer at Verney Junction on 11th. September 1965.

A typical LMR suburban train bound for Marylebone waits in the bay platform at Aylesbury on 16th. August 1960. It is composed of ex-LMS coaches and the loco is Class 4 2-6-4T No.42250. The left-hand water-column is embossed "GWR WOLVERHAMPTON WORKS APRIL 1880".

The last steam-hauled local passenger train northwards from Aylesbury waits to start behind Class 4 2-6-4T No. 42178 on 2nd. March 1963. It was the very last train due to call at Quainton Road.

50

Last one! Class 4 2-6-4T No. 42230 prepares to leave Aylesbury with the very last steam Met. southbound on 9th. September 1961. The driver shows the "Aylesbury's Last Met." artwork.

The last southbound passenger train due to call at Quainton Road, the 4.18 p.m. on 2nd. March 1963. It is running very late and darkness has fallen. 'Black Five' No. 45567 carries a single 'ordinary passenger' headlight. Note the very early Met. Railway sign in ultra-marine enamel.

The last changeover of the Chesham shuttles, on 11th. September 1960. Class 2 2-6-2T No. 41284 propels the train into Chorley Wood.

51

A typical two-coach Princes Risborough train seen at Aylesbury on 16th. December 1950. The leading coach – probably ex-NER – is in the sepia brown used on older stock as a less-common alternative to the plain mid brown usually applied.

The 1 p.m. WR goods to Princes Risborough at Aylesbury on a date in 1951. The use of an ER Class N5 0-6-2T – here No. 69300 – was typical on this train for a short period.

Unusual power for a mid-day goods from the Princes Risborough line. No. 4608 has the road to back into the north yard at Aylesbury on 18th. August 1964. 61XX's were normally used.

52

Chesham goods: 'Black Five' No. 45342 shunts the yard on 27th. November 1964, signalled by a Met. Railway dwarf semaphore. The train is No. 9T06.

The morning goods from Quainton Road, now renumbered 9T07, arrives at Aylesbury on 27th. November 1964. Engine No.76039.

A new destination: BR Standard Class 9 2-10-0 No. 92031 prepares train 6T24 for Northampton in Aylesbury's north goods yard on 14th. August 1964.

Towards the end of the ex-Met. freight service Standard Class 4 2-6-0 No.76035 runs into Aylesbury with a typical goods train on 4th. August 1965. These local trips had by then been incorporated into the LMR train-numbering series – this one was No. 9T02.

Ex-GWR 2-6-2T No. 6167 has arrived light at Aylesbury Town on 30th. July 1964. It has already lost its front number-plate. It is making up a train laden with farm machinery with which it will depart via the GW & GC line later that evening. The train will be No. 7V21.

Like almost all LT locomotives at the time, 0-6-0ST No. L.53 is in immaculate condition as it comes into Willesden Green with a goods train on 16th. August 1955.

Unusual power for No. 10 goods, neither British Railways nor Metropolitan: ex-Underground 0-6-0T No. L.30 drifts back down the Bakerloo road to Neasden with the 1.12. p.m. empties from Willesden Green on 5th. August 1960.

Still enjoying its promotion to revenue-earning service, No. L.30 has arrived at Willesden Green with freight from Neasden and is shunting the coal-wagons. The WR p.w. train is parked on the former goods shed road; the white stumps are all that remains of the shed. The loading gauge was painted light grey. 8th. August 1960.

55

L. 53 shunts Neasden station goods yard, with brake van B.562 in attendance. The tail of a London Brick Co's lorry may just be seen on the left and Charringtons' coal lorries were often in the yard. Taken on 2nd. July 1951.

Ex-Met. Railway Class F 0-6-2T No. L.49 arrives at Willesden Green with No.9 goods on 30th. October 1950. This train left Neasden at 11.25 a.m. and ran when required.

Electric locomotive No.8 "Sherlock Holmes" hurries the Chiltern Court coal train from Neasden to Baker Street through Willesden Green on 6th. September 1957. In the background the small crane and its platform were originally within the goods shed, now demolished.

LT pannier No. L.90 waits at Stoke Mandeville following a visit to Aylesbury on p. way work. 19th. June 1966.

Class L1 2-6-4T No. 67778 awaits the call to duty with a rake of six Dreadnoughts at Aylesbury, while across the tracks LT Class F 0-6-2T No. L.50 awaits a path back to London after running round a p.w. train. The leading brake is ex-Met. No. B.575. The ex-GCR home signals have lost their finials but gained new upper-quadrant arms. 4th. April 1956.

LT tamping machine No. PBT 760 is parked unusually on the former GW & GC side of Aylesbury station. It was finished in pale grey with red lettering. 26th. August 1966.

57

It is a misty Sunday morning as L.44 heads back to Neasden after running round at Aylesbury on 21st. August 1955.

The first time recorded at Aylesbury by the author, ex-GWR 0-6-0 pannier-tank No. 7711 takes water while on trial with LT for p.w. work. Photographed on 22nd. May 1956.

L.95 waits in the bay platform at Aylesbury for an early morning express to pass before returning southwards on 25th. July 1965, during the rebuilding of Euston.

This splendid group of LT engines was taken at Neasden by the late Mr W.C.J. Starling on 1st. September 1953. Until the late fifties it was rare indeed to see any LT engine other than immaculate. The locos are L.49, 48 and 44, with a saddle-tank beyond.

A view from the footbridge of Wendover station goods yard with LT brake No. B.554 parked on a siding. The LNER fencing, LMR lighting and a Met. platform bench may be noted, and there are good supplies of coal in the yard. Photographed on 18th. October 1964.

No. L.91 heads a train of empties from the tip siding round the curve from the Watford line towards the main line at Watford South Junction on 18th. April 1958.

The former Met. & GC crane, painted by LT as No. C.619 in 1954. It was in standard grey with liberal touches of red on dangerous parts and had black underframes. It had no indication of current ownership, merely the "C.619" on the solebars. By the time it was photographed on 2nd. May 1960 the number had been painted out leaving only the old joint ownership shown on embossed plates.

The jib-wagon (J.) 690 with crane C.619 at Harrow. The "J." did not appear on the vehicle, and the number itself was painted out with a white patch within a few years as can be seen, leaving only the 'MET. & GCR JOINT No. 1" plate (with the lettering picked out) as identification. The wagon is grey with red ends and black frames. Photographed on 2nd. May 1960.

Steam crane C.604 photographed at Neasden Depot on 9th. April 1960 shows its black livery with single red lining which can best be seen on the panel bearing the name "LONDON TRANSPORT". Note the unusual presentation with the first word above the second. Both name and number were in gilt.

This heavy crane's jib-wagon, No. J.683, is lined red and lettered and numbered in gilt to match the crane. Taken on 15th. March 1959, the melancholy occasion was the cutting-up of Class F 0-6-2T No. L.50. In contrast, similar jib-wagon No. J.684 was in unlined black and had no lettering, although its number was in gilt and the wagon's ends were painted red.

The number "700" is lost against the red band on this ex-Met. Railway milk-van seen at Neasden as part of the breakdown train on 9th. April 1960.

Wagon No. 704 was one of the LT breakdown vehicles, and was photographed on 9th. April 1960. The gilt lettering on an all-grey vehicle was very unusual. The darker 'background' to the transfers is merely a coat of clear varnish applied over them.

Seen on the Klondyke sidings at Neasden Depot on 14th. May 1966 are 0-6-0PT No. L.95 and brake van B.555, built for LT by Hurst Nelson in 1935. In the background are the power station chimneys.

A typical Sunday morning engineer's train drifts into Rickmansworth behind another pannier, No. L.93, on 21st. August 1960.

63

The BR version of LT brake-van livery is seen here on B.585 with L.96 at Aylesbury on 14th. June 1963. All the lettering on the light grey sides is on black panels, but the numbers on the ends were applied directly to the normal bright red. The vans were later repainted in the standard LT scheme.

A BR p. way train hauled by Class 8F 2-8-0 No. 48654 photographed during the last years of steam. It is actually on the GW and GC line, which from Aylesbury station to the fixed distant (inclusive) 100 yards in the rear of the train was LMR territory; beyond that the WR was in control.

Ex-Met. brake van B.564 is stationed at Wendover for a few days. In the background an LMR 2-6-4T brings a Met. Line train from Aylesbury past a Met. signal and a red LT warning sign. 10th. June 1956.

This LT brake van, No. B.574, parked on Aylesbury's south sidings and photographed during 1947, has a plaque near the right-hand entrance (just visible) reading "FOR USE BETWEEN AYLESBURY AND NEASDEN LNER FOR LONDON TRANSPORT GUARDS".

Typical finish for ballast wagons is shown here; all grey with black frames. Photographed on 9th. April 1960, the wagon had been painted a month earlier. Stencils had been used for the name and number although these were still closely Johnston in form. The number is without the usual full stops, and slight variations can be seen in the arrangement of "LONDON" and "TRANSPORT" between this wagon and its neighbour.

Hopper wagons were always particularly precisely finished with the name in neat, equal-sized letters; no doubt a smooth surface aided the painter. Here is H.W. 407 at Neasden on 9th. April 1960.

65

0-6-0 No. AMW 188 waits for the level crossing gates to open so that it can cross the busy A 413 with goods from Wendover to Halton Camp on 5th. April 1948.

An entrance to the Halton line on the Tring road, Halton – the Upper Icknield Way. Note the coal stored on the left and the weighbridge centre foreground with the office on the right. It is building No. 218, shown in black on a partly hidden white circle. Most of the paintwork is greyish-green and cream. Photographed on 7th. June 1965.

Two of the six gates which guarded the Halton line where it crossed the A 413, photographed on 7th. June 1965. They were still in place in 1996!

A train for Halton approaches the bridge over the Wendover arm of the Grand Union canal on 21st. August 1952.

The rear of the same train taken from the canal bridge a few moments later. The train carries no head- or tail-lamps.

A view of the Halton line looking away from Wendover goods yard. The wooden gradient post looks similar to the early Met. design. Behind the camera were gates across the line and an LTE end-of-maintenance plate. 16th. August 1953.

A loop on the Halton track between Wendover and the A 413 level crossing. Taken on the same date as the picture above.

The Lowlands Road entrance to Harrow-on-the-Hill station on 30th. October 1950. Note the "UNDERGROUND" and "LNER" logos.

The main entrance to Harrow-on-the-Hill station in College Road taken in 1952. Besides the Underground/LNER logos above, the canopy glass reads "METROPOLITAN LINE & LNER" at each end, with logos.

Part of the old creosoted wooden station at Moor Park. The extra large 'bar' of the ring-and-bar which used to show the words "AND SANDY LODGE" in addition may be noted. 20th. April 1961.

69

South of Met. & GC territory but well worth including is this pleasing frontage at Preston Road. The background to the lettering was blackish until painted blue in 1957. The local roads were then safe enough for young cyclists. 16th. June 1950.

Displaying the same style of lettering is the awning at Northwick Park. Above it may be seen an approximation in stone of the Met. diamond logo, but here the diamond overlaps the bar. 18th. April 1958.

On 3rd. August 1960 North Harrow station shows its identity by means of white glass behind a Met. railway stencil painted blue. At nationalisation the joint committee's title appeared on the skyline above, but the masonry displaying it was quickly removed.

The anonymous exterior of Northwood old station as on 4th. November 1958; it was soon to be demolished. A carmine and cream parcels van peeps into the picture on the right.

A thirties-style timetable-display kiosk at the junction of Lowlands Road with the station approach at Harrow-on-the-Hill, still in place on 2nd. April 1984.

The paintwork at Quainton Road on 26th. March 1948 is all wartime grey. The station is now purely Eastern Region, and some of the LT poster-headings are already being removed – revealing "METROPOLITAN" beneath! It will, however, still be served by two LT trains daily for a further two months.

The far building at Verney Junction on 7th. February 1965, in LMR gulf red and cream with dark red signs with screwed-on letters.

Verney Junction as seen from the signal box on 11th. September 1965.

A DMU from the Oxford direction passes Verney Junction box as it approaches the station on 31st. July 1959. A man waits to cross the line but no passengers await the train.

The platform road in this view of Verney Junction was formerly used by the Met. trains. It was taken on the same date as the picture above. Everything slumbers but the weeds and the porter.

A comprehensive sign at Watford photographed on 5th. January 1951.

Soon it had been replaced by this much simpler sign, typical of the modern frameless, rounded cornered type which also shows well the sharp two-feathered arrow in use at the time.

Publicity at Wendover station approach on 22nd. April 1968. The embankment has been landscaped following the installation of a pedestrian footbridge. The Met. and GC sign, relocated from dense undergrowth nearby, soon disappeared.

A later photograph (7th. April 1983) to show the modest station name-box fitted over the front entrance at Amersham and other LT stations at the time of Met. modernisation. The box displays both the LT roundel and the BR 'double arrow' symbols.

The entrance to Aylesbury station – "TOWN" to distinguish between it and the former LNWR station which was appended "HIGH STREET". Note the very large maroon sign over the traditional entrance. The parcels office entrance straight ahead became the main entrance for a period subsequently, but as the regular service to London continued to use the bay platform near the old entrance, passengers had a much longer walk from booking office to trains, and the original arrangement was restored. 1st. August 1965.

Apart from one poster-heading in LMR maroon the frontage of Quainton Road is quite anonymous on 6th. August 1959. All other poster – headings have been removed. The lamp bore the overpainted name "WEST WYCOMBE" in the glass! The premises are in the current LMR gulf red and cream scheme.

76

Two ragwort plants have selfset artistically flanking one of the ring-and-bars at Harrow. These pre-war signs have fine black outlines to the red ring, with a further thin white outline just within the bronze frame. The story goes that a strain of ragwort was brought from its home among Italian lava to Oxford for study. Seeds escaped onto the GWR's lava-like ballast along which the slipstream of trains spread the plant to many parts – it's quicker by rail. Photograph: May 1988.

One of the last Met. diamond nameboards at Northwood Hills on 30th. October 1950. The diamond was red, and the bar blue. The outermost frame to the white square was station brown, with an inner moulding of dark blue. The last of these signs had gone by early January 1951.

The last Met. sign with black-shaded white letters on a bright red ground, photographed on 6th. November 1948, three days before it was removed. Rings-and-bars on angle-iron frames then became standard. Even Amersham still retained some gas lights at this early date.

77

One of these small plates (BELOW) was the only permanent LT sign to be seen north of Stoke Mandeville. It was fixed to the platform building at Aylesbury, and was in cream, lettered black; the ring-and-bar was red/blue.

One of the lamp-tablets from Aylesbury (ABOVE) put up by the LNER after the war. They remained in position until the advent of LMR maroon totems. They are in the dark blue that was to have become LNER standard – and did on the Eastern Region – but the lettering is pure London Transport. An LNER poster-heading plate is shown beneath for comparison which is in perfect Gill Sans. Compare the "E" in both plates; that in "AYLESBURY' has unequal strokes.

BELOW LEFT: Obsolete for twelve years, this sign at Verney Junction was still in LMS black and white when photographed on 7th. August 1948. When eventually repainted in LMR maroon the last line was not picked out. The whole sign had disappeared by July 1965.

RIGHT: One of the standard signs provided at this station. They were its only identification as no totems were ever put up. Photographed on 2nd. October 1965.

78

A shot showing the bedraggled look of Wendover station in the remains of its wartime grey before the first repaint by LT in 1952. It was identical in appearance to its two immediate neighbours. The drabness is relieved only by white anti-blackout bands on the pillars and possibly stone colour under the canopies.

The Great Missenden – Stoke Mandeville group of stations had duplicate sets of buildings on the down platforms until after the LMR takeover in 1961 when they were demolished. The buildings at Great Missenden shown here on 18th. January 1964 had already been equipped with standard dark red LMR totems and other signs despite their impending doom. Premises still in LT's 'old' colours. The up buildings were soon to be repainted by LT in a non-standard scheme.

As was so often the case at country stations a lone poster-heading plate is the only identification at Verney Junction, taken on 7th. January 1965. This is the only entrance, though the combined booking office is out of use and tickets are sold from a window on the platform.

79

The two-road Great Western engine-shed at Aylesbury. Besides a GWR "NO ADMITTANCE" sign the front bears a standard red-and-white "WARNING LIMITED CLEARANCE" chequerboard (these could also be seen on the nearby coaling-stage and at various bridges up the line) and a sign warning against excessive smoke emission. It is lettered in maroon on white, with a yellow panel at the top bearing the word "WARNING" in black. The coal-stage also had a non-standard "LIMITED CLEARANCE" board painted with white letters on dark red; it was on a gulf-red post. The shed was photographed on 17th. June 1962 and demolished in November 1967.

ABOVE: Like those at Wendover and Stoke Mandeville, the down platform buildings at Great Missenden are being demolished to be replaced by a small wooden 'bus shelter'. Some of the maroon signs have yet to be removed. The footbridge is painted in LT's greenish-bluish bridge grey. Bridge plate MR 128 is white on black with white frame. 15th. February 1964.

LEFT: The announcement of the end at Quainton Road. The poster speaks for itself on 18th. June 1966.

The fine set of LT signs at Willesden Green goods yard. London Transport told me that they dated from about 1936, and are here seen on the 1st. September 1959. The corrugated iron building is tarred, and the paintwork is cream and deep blue-green, replaced after the BR takeover by Charrington's green-bice and deep cream.

A lorry on the new weighbridge at Willesden Green on 22nd. February 1965. A new window has replaced the two original ones and the "GOODS OFFICE" sign has been removed from the fanlight over the door to the new office nearby.

When the coal traffic to Willesden Green was considerably increased in mid-1962 and the old goods office taken over by Charringtons this new cedarwood structure – a garden-shed de luxe – was erected on the platform that had originally been within the corrugated iron goods shed, and the goods office sign was transferred to the new building. All the paintwork is emerald green. Taken on 10th. July 1962; only three and a half years were to elapse before the yard closed altogether.

Almost joint to the end: London Transport owns Willesden Green depot but the London Midland Region closes it on 3rd. January 1966. Alternative facilities will be available at Willesden Junction. Photographed five days before closure.

The Met. Line has been modernised and DMU's and other fasts run behind Pinner hidden by the new brick wall, but, looking anachronistic, a loose-coupled goods hauled by Standard 2-6-0 No. 76037 still rumbles through the station during the twilight of the ex-Met. freight service. 14th. September 1964.

Almost lost against the model shop's enthusiastic display is the compromise sign at Harrow-on-the-Hill goods yard. Although in correct LT Johnston lettering it is lettered "BRITISH RAILWAYS". Flag black on white with pale grey frame, post mid grey. The speed limit sign is white on red, the "NO PARKING' one is blue on white, and the gates are silver. 13th. August 1965.

A colourful sign on the gates of Croxley goods yard, seen on 3rd. January 1966. Upper half white on red, the lower olive green on cream.

A close-up of the classic LT goods office sign from Willesden Green, showing the high-quality teak framing typical of these pre-war signs.

83

Harrow-on-the-Hill's goods shed and weighbridge office on 3rd. April 1967. The poster on the door announces closure on that very day, and states that alternative facilities will be available at Cricklewood. The fruiterer's sign is believed to be in black-shaded red on yellow.

Harrow-on-the-Hill's goods office on 19th. April 1968. The paintwork is still grey and cream as before closure.

LT's reluctant provision of goods facilities led to the painting of some interesting signs for which they had no standard enamels. This sign (seen on the railings above) was in black on white with a cream frame. Taken on the same date.

This weighbridge office at Amersham with its round-topped windows is a typical Met. Railway design. It still retains its weighbridge but the office has been taken over by the "Evening News" as the door-sign shows. Photographed on 17th. August 1959.

The entrance to Pinner goods yard, anonymous like so many on the line. The weighbridge office, which is similar to that at Chalfont (q.v.), looks semi-derelict although the weighbridge is still in position. The "5 M.P.H. IN GOODS YARD" sign in red on white adds a little brightness. Taken on 29th. June 1967.

Wembley Park weighbridge office shows evidence of two of its many owners – brown and cream Western Region paintwork and the familiar Metropolitan red "NO VEHICLES..." sign. At the time of the photograph the plate again reads "METROPOLITAN RAILWAY', though this heading had been overpainted "LNER" in a simpler style when that railway took over. Photographed during 1957.

85

Great Missenden goods yard entrance three months after closure: grey gates and maroon LMR sign, and Met. weighhouse with cream 1959 window and sickly green door, as painted by LT in 1963. The new window is similar to that at Chesham. 2nd. October 1966.

All is neat and tidy at Amersham yard on 17th. August 1959 where the cattle-dock with its gas-lamp strikes an old time note. A carmine and cream mechanical horse trailer may be glimpsed behind it and the Met. Railway down home signal leans into the picture on the right. The dark rectangle above it is the end of the temporary up starter's semaphore. The buffer stop strangely appears to be of LNER type, its 'beam' comprising three lengths of rail. As at the passenger station, the doors and window frames are dull green and cream respectively.

The goods shed at Chesham on 22nd. May 1955. The white-lettered grey board reads "GOODS OFFICE LONDON MIDLAND REGION CHESHAM".

This shot taken on 30th. October 1950 shows the goods shed at Willesden Green, soon to disappear. It is of corrugated iron and painted all over brown.

A later use of the old Metropolitan Railway style of sign with black-shaded white letters on a vermilion ground. Photographed on 22nd. February 1965 at Watford goods yard, originally Met. Railway and LNER joint.

Commuters seem unperturbed by the demolition of Pinner's goods shed proceeding behind them on 31st. October 1960. Northwood's shed was generally similar but had round windows facing the running lines.

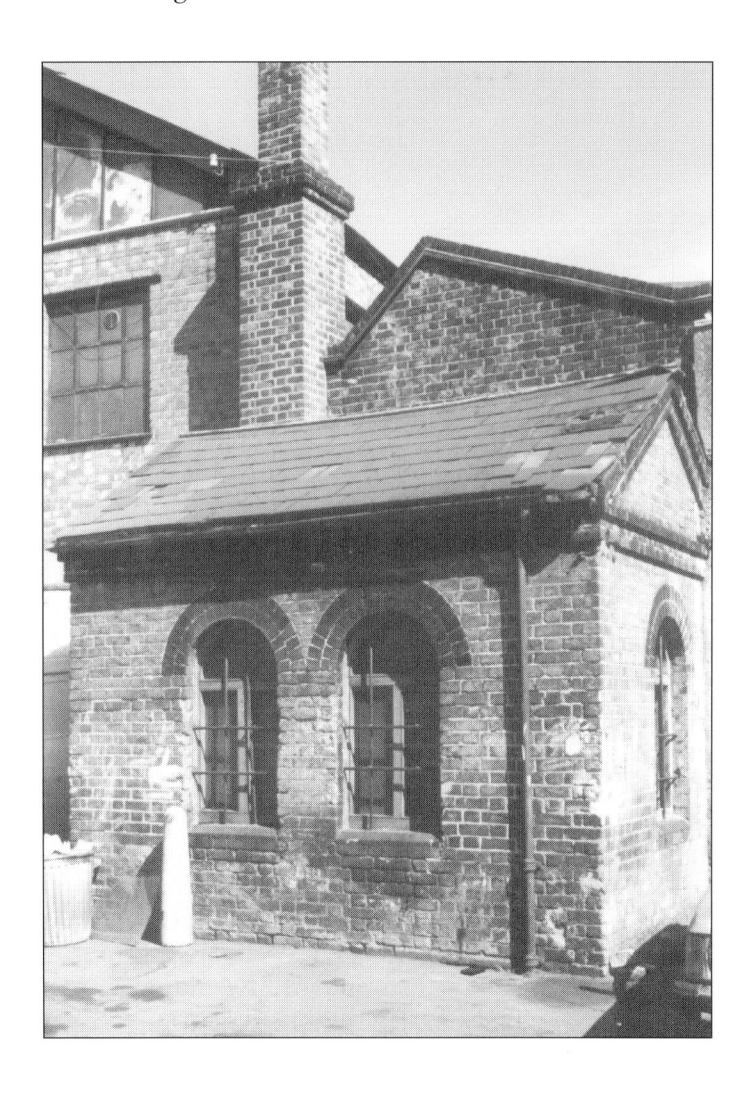

Remarkably still standing on 31st. May 1985 is the Met. weighbridge office at Finchley Road, at that time used by a motor firm.

LMS-designed 2-6-4T No. 42256 has a good head of steam as she shunts at Chesham controlled by some attractive miniature and ground signals of Met. Railway origin. 25th. May 1961.

On 17th. August 1959 there is plenty of spare land around Amersham goods shed. Goods awaiting transit may be glimpsed through the open doors. Notice the standard Met. Railway sign, black on white. In earlier days the "CAUTION" was sometimes picked out in red.

The goods office at Neasden station. It had been dark brown overall from 1949 when a plain black-on-white board reading "LTE GOODS OFFICE" had been affixed between the window and the porch. By 3rd. January 1966 the hut had acquired 'modern' colours (mid grey, cream windows, black pipework) but its board had come off. It was still propped against the inside wall of the porch.

Chorley Wood's goods yard viewed from the footbridge across it on 25th. August 1960. Part of the bridge was later retained to carry cables.

At the anonymous entrance to Chalfont goods yard can be seen the mainly wooden weighbridge office which has already lost its "4 TONS" sign. The body is cream, door mid blue, pipes black. Note also the typical LT rail-built buffer stop, and the non-standard wooden example behind. Both have their typical white touches to the red. The porter's barrow looks a little out-of-place between the stops. 15th. April 1967.

The basic goods yard at Stoke Mandeville on 29th. July 1965 – a single siding and a solitary sign. The shadow is cast by a small goods shed.

The remains of the gasworks spur at South Harrow, curving left away from the Piccadilly Line. The track had been taken up by early 1958. View taken on 19th. May 1985 from alongside the bridge carrying the line over Roxeth Green Avenue.

The Brill Branch at Quainton Road sees a train again on 7th. April 1964 as No. 76039 shunts an afternoon freight.

A panorama of Aylesbury Town goods yard, showing the large goods shed and office, covered cattle-pens, diesel shunter and train 1D33, an uncommon use of a DMU on one of the remaining services north of Aylesbury. Photographed on 3rd. September 1966, the date of their withdrawal.

A wagon stands at the new coal concentration depot north of Aylesbury on 20th. June 1966. The sign is correct LMR dark red but has non-standard lettering. In the left background can be seen the International Alloys factory whose siding left the main line a short distance away.

A new depot established towards the end of our period was this oil depot leading from Aylesbury's north yard. It was not photographed until 4th. April 1983.

A rather sorry-looking gas lamp on the platform fence at Wendover. As electric lighting had not been installed at the time of the platform extensions for the new diesel trains, several NEW gas lights were provided on the lengthened platforms in the interim. Behind the lamp can be seen one of the first world war utility huts that served in many capacities after the war. For many years this example was the station café, with access both from the road and from the up platform. 15th. February 1964.

New lamps for old – gas and fluorescence happily co-exist in the station approach at Wendover. The gas lamp was removed in February 1965. Photographed on 15th. September 1964.

Although the passenger facilities at Wendover were electrically lit soon after dieselisation, gas lingered on in the signal box for many years – this shot was not taken until late 1983!

93

Two examples of the oil lamp design by Silber, Fleming of London which was at one time very common at the ex-Met. stations.

Oil lighting survived until the end at Verney Junction. This lamp on the footbridge was photographed on the day before closure, 29th. December 1967.

Wembley Park's modern-looking signal box, with vintage signs in black seriffed letters on white seen on 6th. September 1957. In 1948 the passenger station still had its old diamond nameboards. With the forthcoming Olympic Games in mind they were modernised by painting out the red triangles and replacing them with segments of red rings. The original bars, with their by now non-standard lettering, were retained.

An interesting signal at Northwood, with dolls numbered from left to right E16, E13 and E8. The last-named has been preserved. The box is light grey and cream, with its nameboard cream with black letters. A Western Region p.w. train is parked in the goods yard. Photograph: 19th. August 1959.

Croxley signal box on 3rd. January 1966. The box is finished in dull bluish-green and cream, and although it still has its Met. nameboard on the front the name has not been applied. Below the number plate of signal B 19 can be seen one of the fairly new disc-distants put in during the early sixties to allow extra braking distance for freight trains. The plate below it, yellow like the disc, is not numbered but is labelled "WATFORD NORTHBOUND DISTANT".

Chorley Wood box on 8th. October 1959, with its quaint 'old fashioned' expanded lettering. The box is in cream with mid grey frames. The board is black on cream. No. 10 goods shunts in the background.

Chorley Wood's new signal box "JS", brick-built at the time of the Met. modernisation, displays a standard blue-on-white sign. The old box, repainted overall light grey with ivory window frames in 1960, still carries its old wooden board, now lettered in black in near-Johnston on ivory. Taken on 29th. June 1967; the yard was closed earlier that year.

The Met. signal box at Amersham with its successor being built in the background. The old box is painted cream with light grey framing. 17th. August 1959.

Chesham signal box on 17th. August 1959. It is finished in dark and light grey and the board is lettered in black on white.

Great Missenden's Metropolitan box has been repainted by LT for the second time in three years. The body is light grey with ivory window frames, and the doors are black. The warning sign is in LMR maroon enamel, but the LNER nameboards have again been repainted in the persistent LNER style of white on black. They continued thus until the box closed; they were never maroon. The Met. milepost M29 has been repainted in LT style in white with black base. At later repaints the "M" was omitted. 15th. February 1964.

Wendover signal box, repainted in the 'old' colours (brown and cream) by LT prior to the LMR take-over – and repainted by LT in 1963 in the grey scheme also seen at Great Missenden (q.v.). 10th. October 1961.

This signal box-like structure at Aylesbury was used as a p.w. hut at the time of photography which was 8th. August 1965. The station manager at the time referred to it as the "old local box".

Aylesbury North box, with the commodious goods shed behind. Taken on 13th. February 1965 still in its LMR gulf red/cream scheme with crimson and white board, it would be demolished within three years.

The South box at Aylesbury, retained and repainted in the later dull olive and cream scheme, again with dark red board, and seen on 13th. February 1965.

The large Met. signal box at Quainton Road, demolished by February 1968. One of its LNER nameboards was preserved and has gone back to Quainton for installation on the new preserved signal box. Date: 31st. March 1964.

The signal box at Verney Junction passenger station. Its LMS board is in standard white on dark red; the body is gulf red and cream. 7th. February 1965.

This large gong was to be seen on the eastbound platform at Verney Junction. It is painted dark brown. 4th. June 1967.

The post of the Great Missenden down distant, dated 10-4-18 and heavily strapped round with angle-iron where the concrete is crumbling, has a "GREAT MISSENDEN 29" plate. The fishtail is sharp-pointed, unlike a true GC arm. View taken on 11th. June 1964.

BELOW: A temporary up starter signal at Amersham. It has a tubular steel post and a fluted enamel blade which appears to be a reused one from a withdrawn District Line signal. An expert on LT affairs has doubted that LT made use of second-hand components, but how otherwise does one explain the use of an electrical box by the lineside near Moor Park which was embossed 'LCC TRAMWAYS 1913"? Photograph 30th. August 1957.

The down starter at Great Missenden has been overhauled by LT. Its ex-GCR arm now tapers towards the tip instead of vice-versa and two rather large notches deface the arm; they accommodate a brace on the back. This signal, as with a few others at this station, has acquired an LT enamel plate "GREAT MISSENDEN 27" in black on white. The concrete post renders the signal inconspicuous against the concrete of the bridge. Note the standard LMR maroon warning sign. The redundant bridge No. MR 130, seen in the distance, was blown up appropriately enough on 5th. November 1967. Photo 18th. January 1964.

Great Missenden up distant's arm tapers with a delicate curve from root to tip. It has a perforated ball to its spiked finial, but otherwise is of GC style; one component is however marked "Met. Rly. 40". Across the line may be seen one of the single aspect mechanical colour lights. Seen on 11th. June 1964.

The up home at Great Missenden, a thoroughbred GC signal. 11th. June 1964.

The lofty advanced starter at Great Missenden. The arm lacks the rounded corners of a true GC signal. Photograph: 15th. February 1964.

103

Wendover's up distant. The arm does not appear to be original as it lacks the characteristic radiused corners which GC arms had even on distants. Repainted by LMR with white post and finial and viewed on 15th. June 1964.

The up starter signal at Wendover, a mechanical colour-light. The GCR/LNER "works" had been transferred to a reused Met. post at the time of the platform extensions to accommodate the longer DMUs. The signal is showing single yellow in the upper aspect (note the upper quadrant stub in the inclined position), while the lower is blank. Photograph: 15th. June 1964.

The refuge signal at Wendover. It has an ancient Met. arm, though the post has been Great Centralised with a ball-and-spike finial. During World War II recent paint had weathered off, leaving the arm vermilion with a *black* stripe, a very old Met. practice. For years this post was enveloped in a wooden platform extension which had recently been removed (see Page 64); the post now displays more black paint then white! The arm is known to have been preserved. 21st. June 1964.

104

The advanced starter at Wendover beautifully renovated by London Transport. It has acquired what looks like an ex-District enamelled arm, unfluted. The post has been meticulously painted in silver with black details. A nearby cabinet is in station brown with black roof. The signal later received an old Met. wooden arm, then a standard upper quadrant one in November 1963, and by 6th. July 1964 a completely new upper quadrant signal had replaced it. Photographed on 16th. August 1953.

This all-metal signal guards the exit from Aylesbury locoshed. A similar one could be seen at Marylebone, though the latter's arm managed to incorporate a white stripe of minimum breadth. Taken on 17th. September 1966.

This GCR signal guards the Halton Camp line exit at the north end of Wendover goods yard. London Transport had abandoned black bases by the signal's last repaint and the post is all-silver. It was photographed on 15th. June 1964.

105

The backing signal at Quainton Road. Further GC signals and the Met. box may be seen in the distance, and an LNER ¼ milepost (44¼ miles from Baker Street) nearby. The train is No. 10 goods, shown in the BR working timetable as "LT from Quainton Road". 6th. August 1959.

An interesting group of GC and Met. signals at Verney Junction taken on 24th. August 1956, before the goods yard was remodelled into storage sidings. Two of the Met. arms on the left have lost their balancing blades. They had been all red with white stripes, lacking the black parts. Compare with Wendover refuge signal. The posts are still wartime grey with short black bases.

A good Met. Railway signal at Chesham goods yard on 27th. March 1964.

Exit from the north end of Stoke Mandeville yard was controlled by this Met. Railway signal. Originally a semaphore type, it had been fitted typically with a rather large enamel disc. This signal, and another identical one, are believed to have been put in during 1951 after the LT takeover. Apart from the disc, the signal is by this date in overall LMR black. A Southern-type concrete hut stands by the down platform, but its companion larger hut has been replaced by a 'garden shed'. 7th. June 1965.

This dolly-signal controlled the entrance to Stoke Mandeville siding from the south end. The lamp casing is stamped GCR but the lever has gained an LNE-C weight; this hybridisation among signals was common. The signal has recently been repainted in meticulous LT style with every bolt-head picked out against the wooden base. The metalwork is all silver, with red and white disc. Date: 1953.

A modernised type of LNER revolving disc-signal seen in Wendover goods yard on 29th. July 1965.

107

The writing is already on the wall for the parcels service, as the poster announces its withdrawal from Amersham, Chesham, Great Missenden, Stoke Mandeville and Wendover on 'our' line. On 15th. April 1966 light bulbs are seen being handled at the latter station. Note the interesting barrows, and the new LMR striplighting. LT have repainted the station in non-standard colours although the white and black-edged posterboards, without headings, show the standard LT finish of the time.

A yellow-painted parcels van calls at Harrow-on-the-Hill three days before closure of the parcels office. Taken on 25th. February 1966. The van is No. 1634D-M.

Parcels are unloaded from the shuttle at Chesham on 23rd. May 1950.

108

A former vehicular crossing of the line – one of several – north of Amersham but still in LT territory. Pipework dives underground between the gate and the track, but vehicles would have found passage difficult as no sleepers are provided between the lines. 8th. March 1987.

A footpath crosssing just in LMR territory north of Amersham. LT pipework rises in a bridge to allow pedestrian passage. 8th. March 1987.

This handsome "WAY OUT" sign, in blue with red ring on white, is of the type standard on LT stations from the fifties until a simplified arrow was brought into use in 1968. Taken at Rickmansworth on 25th. May 1996.

Two of these old-fashioned looking painted boards were in use at North Harrow until standard enamel signs came along. The lettering is off-white, shaded black, on brown stipple.

This venerable blue sign at Neasden station could be one of the originals from the early days of the line. It did not disappear until about the late eighties, so could have achieved its century. Photographed on 24th. April 1983.

A clear sign in non-standard serif lettering at North Harrow. It is presumably a Metropolitan provision and has blue lettering. The date is 3rd. August 1960.

110

Still in place at Moor Park on 30th. October 1950, this red, white and black PAINTED sign appears to be a Met. Railway survival. Old photographs show that it was certainly in place in 1934.

Private road sign at Rickmansworth. It is enamelled with blue lettering on a cream ground, normal for these signs. Taken about 1959.

This sign with its quaint lettering stands in the station approach at Amersham, and is the only one of its type seen by the author. Photographed: 4th. April 1966.

This type of GCR "BEWARE..." sign could be seen at the many farm crossings from Aylesbury exclusive almost to Verney Junction, and with a "GW & GC" heading, at Aylesbury itself. These signs remained in the black and white scheme shown, irrespective of changes of ownership.

A close-up shot of a type of GC sign that was common at many locations between Great Missenden and the Verney Junction branch. It shows a typical LNER finish, perpetuated by London Transport on their newly-acquired section, for instance at Stoke Mandeville goods yard, 1952-55.

This fine close-up shot by Mr. Brian Leslie shows the signs at a foot-crossing near Chalfont and Latimer, replaced by a footbridge when electrification came in. It was taken on 15th. March 1959, and shows a pure Met. "BEWARE..." sign and a "...FORTY SHILLING..." (believed ex-GCR) below. The latter was the only type of sign to be seen both sides of the old LT/LNER boundary at Great Missenden.

112

The only one of these signs bearing the Met.'s full title seen on the line by the writer. It is seen at Northwood on 30th. October 1950. Always black on white during the period, others existed that lacked the title; these were usually in white on red. Specimens could be seen in the Rickmansworth – Watford area.

A foot-crossing over the 'pure' ex-GC line a mile north of Quainton Road Junction – then why has it a full set of four Met. & GC beware/trespass plates? No. 45416 approaches on the 2.38 p.m. from Marylebone. Photographed on 11th. July 1964.

This very old "PASSENGERS MUST NOT..." sign at Quainton Road was in white on blue and bore the Met. Railway's title in full in tiny letters in the bottom left-hand corner. Photographed in 1951.

113

This notice, photographed after preservation, used to be displayed on a rail-wagon weighbridge situated at the London end of Aylesbury's coal yard on the south side of the station. Photographed by Mr J. F. B. Stevens.

A close-up of one of the Met. Railway weighbridge plates. After the war it is believed that only two examples were left that had the simple "METROPOLITAN RAILWAY" heading; most, as far out as Wendover, had "METROPOLITAN & GT CENTRAL RLY JT CTEE". The example shown has been painted up to show approximately how the sign at Wembley Park looked after the title had been overpainted.

One of the few standard LT signs to appear on its Great Missenden – Stoke Mandeville line after nationalisation. South of Great Missenden, it had been painted by the LMR in all over black except for the double-sided 'flag' when photographed in February 1973. In LT days its frame was white; on the section that had always been LT the frames were at one time varnished, but most came to be bright red.

This post giving exact distances from Manchester and from Baker Street was put in at the site of Quainton Road Junction after the Verney line junction had been taken out. The distances are 161 miles, 1099 yards and 44 miles, 1048 yards respectively. Photographed on 5th. March 1966.

A catch points sign between Aylesbury and Stoke Mandeville with an odd mixture of serif- and non-serif letters. Similar boards could be seen between Stoke Mandeville and Wendover, and, out of our orbit, between Grendon Underwood and Ashendon Junction on the 'pure' ex-GC line.
Photograph: 28th. February 1981.

115

The new standard style of LT bridge plate first seen by the writer at Chalfont in July 1963. This example is at Amersham, and was photographed on 12th. February 1983.

A standard Metropolitan Railway bridge number-plate on the footbridge at Wendover. It is painted in the LT scheme of the early sixties, when the photograph was taken.

The LNWR bridge plate on Verney Junction's footbridge. Several of this style but with BR initials appeared on bridges between Quainton Road and Aylesbury inclusive, but never south of that point. Most of the plates soon disappeared. Taken on 12th. February 1967.

Milepost 28½ south of Great Missenden – the division of maintenance between the Met./LT and the GCR/LNER until nationalisation. Behind it stood a diamond-shaped board lettered to that effect. Note that until it was withdrawn in the nineties the milepost still retained its raised characters on the Met. side, and was flush-surfaced with signwritten "½" on the other. The LT p.w. marker has commendably correct Johnston numerals moulded into the concrete bar. 3rd. September 1982.

Met. Railway milepost just south of Wendover. Only one of these posts north of Great Missenden received screwed-on numerals; the others had to be carefully signwritten. The milepost is yellow, the p.w. sign put in by LT is white with a black post as painted by the LMR, for it was not photographed until 2nd. September 1982.

The northernmost example of this Met. Railway style of milepost, found just south of Aylesbury. It was the only one of its type to receive small screwed-on LMR numerals. 4th. April 1983.

117

An LNER gradient sign behind Wendover platform, with large and legible characters. Photographed (still in LT paint) on 27th. February 1971.

A standard LT "STOP" board, white on vermilion. They were not numerous on our line; there were a couple in Harrow goods yard and this one is at Rickmansworth. Frames could be black, silver or red. Photographed on 21st. May 1994.

This LT division of maintenance post between Stoke Mandeville and Aylesbury was still in situ when the LMR repainted most local lineside signs in 1971, although by that date it no longer applied. The post is on the down side of the tracks; on the up side was a wooden LMR post which was very short-lived. By the end of the 1948-68 period the division of maintenance was near M.P. 25¼ north of Amersham. Photographed on 7th. March 1981.

The grounded coach-body at Harrow-on-the-Hill yard is seen on 19th. April 1968. It was previously lettered "C & W EXAMINERS No. 257" in lemon on its tan paintwork, but was otherwise anonymous.

A closer view of the old body taken at the same time. It was not broken up until 23rd. October 1971, when it yielded some useful panels of teak for D.I.Y. purposes!

Seen across the staff allotments at Aylesbury on 16th. August 1960 is the body of Met. Railway coach No.212 of 1881. When one of the roads of the locoshed (just out of the picture on the left) needed to be extended through the rear wall of the shed in 1955, 212's body was moved some ten feet sideways. An unidentified ex-LMS 2-6-0 is stabled on this extension. A Met. train at the bay platform can just be seen through the gap.

The guard's end of coach No.212 is seen in close-up on 17th. September 1966. It was broken up by December 1967, when a door was rescued, restored and taken to Quainton's museum.

MR 198, the highest numbered bridge from Baker Street. It carried the line over the road from Winslow near Verney Junction. Photographed on 9th. April 1964, it had been demolished by February 1967.

A bridge on the former Verney Junction branch south of Granborough Road seen on 31st. January 1965. The main structure is of red brick but the parapet is of blue Staffords. This bridge and others were being replaced by embankments in the early seventies.

Bridge MR 160, carrying the A 418 Aylesbury to Oxford road over the line north of Aylesbury. It is very similar to the GWR bridge at Culham. It was taken on 4th. July 1964 and still exists today (2000) but is shortly to be rebuilt.

121

A typical scene on the Quainton Road – Verney Junction line as it appeared in 1953. Note the single line, still in position right through, the traditional platelayers' hut and the "METN & GT CENTL RLY" notice from which the white lettering has weathered off. The object bottom right is the top of a wooden 'cat's ladder' which lifted pedestrians over the fence where there was no break in the wires. Many of the bridges on this line, like (Shipton) Lee Bridge shown in the picture, had a red-brick main structure but the parapets had been rebuilt in Stafford blue bricks.

A traditional platelayers' hut near bridge MR 133 between Great Missenden and Wendover, not photographed until 3rd. January 1986.

The former railwayman's house at the site of Granborough Road station on the Quainton Road – Verney Junction line as seen on 12th. February 1967. It has since been demolished, but others still exist at the time of writing. It could well have been a survivor from A&BR days.

This condemned stock is stabled at a lonely spot between Winslow Road and Verney Junction on the former down line. The "BEWARE OF THE TRAINS" sign is a standard type for the line, but the "METN & GC RY" heading is slightly bolder than usual. Seen on 27th October 1963.

Brook Street, Aylesbury: the approach to the temporary Met. station entrance 1892-94. In the distance is the busy A 413 Aylesbury-Wendover-London road. Had Aylesbury's railway prehistory turned out differently, a link line from the LNWR Cheddington branch would have crossed the A 413 and come approximately along the line of Brook Street before sweeping round to join the Aylesbury and Buckingham Railway at what became the joint station. Happily for today's traffic on the A 413, the A&BR was joined to the Wycombe route instead. Note the derelict gas lamp on the left; there was another within the coal yard behind the camera, but it was moved when the yard was extended following the closure of High Street station. Railwaymen live in the houses on the right. Photographed on 17th. September 1966, since when Brook Street has disappeared under modern development.

A 'Black Five'-hauled train crosses the unmarked parish boundary from Stoke Mandeville into Wendover near culvert MR 150 on 7th. May 1966.

PART 2

STOKE MANDEVILLE

A MET. AND GC STATION IN DETAIL

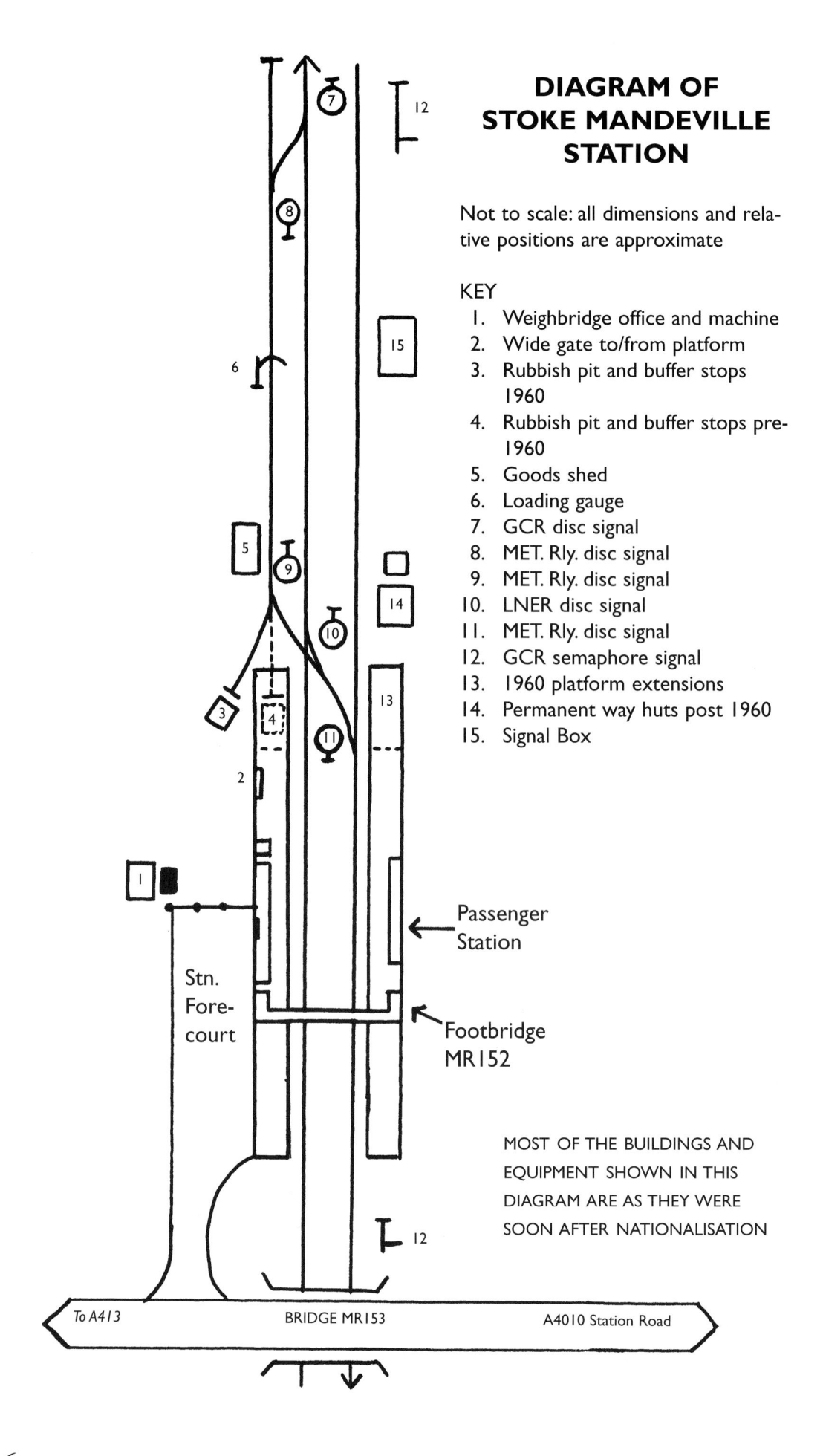

DIAGRAM OF STOKE MANDEVILLE STATION

Not to scale: all dimensions and relative positions are approximate

KEY
1. Weighbridge office and machine
2. Wide gate to/from platform
3. Rubbish pit and buffer stops 1960
4. Rubbish pit and buffer stops pre-1960
5. Goods shed
6. Loading gauge
7. GCR disc signal
8. MET. Rly. disc signal
9. MET. Rly. disc signal
10. LNER disc signal
11. MET. Rly. disc signal
12. GCR semaphore signal
13. 1960 platform extensions
14. Permanent way huts post 1960
15. Signal Box

Passenger Station

Stn. Forecourt

Footbridge MR152

MOST OF THE BUILDINGS AND EQUIPMENT SHOWN IN THIS DIAGRAM ARE AS THEY WERE SOON AFTER NATIONALISATION

To A413   BRIDGE MR153   A4010 Station Road

STOKE MANDEVILLE STATION

Stoke Mandeville station was opened In 1892. It is the first station from Aylesbury on Chiltern Railways' line to London via Amersham. I first made its acquaintance as a youthful train-spotter living in Aylesbury where there was always much railway activity in urban surroundings. Stoke, however, had the advantage of a pleasant country setting, and was a frequently-chosen destination for cycle-rides with friends or walks accompanied by parents, when the return journey would be by train.

Stoke Mandeville has been staffed over the years by keen railwaymen who have done much for the station and its passengers above and beyond the call of duty – Fred Allen, Bert Spittles and Alfred Sanderson, to name but a few from former years – and happily the tradition has continued to the present time when the station is in the care of Alex Mitchell. The station flourishes, and besides its commuters serves folk bound for other local stations on their way to work, school or travelling for pleasure.

THE STOKE MANDEVILLE TRAIN SERVICE

Just before nationalisation most of the passenger trains calling at the station had been provided by the LPTB, which had officially adopted the name Metropolitan Line for its services previously run by the Met. Railway. Most of these trains originated in the City or at Baker Street and terminated at Aylesbury. Many were semi-fast south of Moor Park but called at all stations north of that station. Electrically hauled from London, the trains were steam-hauled by the LNER north of Rickmansworth. In addition to these LPTB trains, there were other stopping and semi-fast trains and a few expresses from the north to Marylebone which did not call at Stoke. All these trains were run by the LNER, later by British Railways Eastern or London Midland Regions according to period. Our station also saw goods trains, which called as required to serve the small single-siding goods yard south east of the passenger station. Throughout most of our period there was one daily working from the Wendover direction only, which called if required. Any traffic originating at Aylesbury or beyond had to be carried through to Wendover earlier and returned to Stoke by this solitary train. The operating department knew it as No.1 Goods, later as No.8A and finally it became No.9T08. The signals on the approach from Wendover were normally kept at "line clear", but if the goods train was required to call at Stoke, the signalman would return his signals to danger on the approach of the train until it was almost upon them, then clear them, allowing the train to draw slowly forward to the passenger platform and then to back into the goods yard to work as required. Notices were posted in the station indicating that the goods service would cease on 5th. July 1965, and that the parcels service would be withdrawn on 14th. April 1966.

In addition to passenger and goods trains, engineers' trains came to Stoke when necessary for maintenance purposes. At the time of nationalisation these trains were based at one of the former GCR depots.

After 1st. January 1948 little difference could be seen in the trains or stations; it was some time before "BRITISH RAILWAYS" appeared on rolling-stock. An administrative alteration at that time was that London Transport would take over maintenance of the Aylesbury line as far north as a point opposite Stoke Mandeville Hospital. Thus after arrears of maintenance had been made up, the ex-LNER engineers' trains (often hauled by ex-Great Central Class J11 0-6-0's) were no longer seen. Their place was taken by trains hauled by the smart maroon locomotives of the London Transport Executive based at Neasden Depot. One of their early tasks was the rerailing of a parcels van which had left the track near Nash Lee Road bridge, No. MR 149.

A major change to Stoke's passenger service occurred after the last London Transport steam passenger service ran on 9th. September 1961. The final departure from Aylesbury for Stoke and

London was accompanied by mournful hooting from the locomotive and by the explosion of detonators placed on the track. The very last LT steam passenger train to call at Stoke arrived from London in the small hours of the next morning, the loco again adorned with unofficial farewell notices, and it terminated at Aylesbury after more subdued hooting. Thereafter diesels took over the service (partially until 1962) and London Transport passenger trains came no nearer than Amersham. Even then Stoke Mandeville had not seen its last steam passenger train, for on 27th. October 1965 a train on the remaining Marylebone – Nottingham longer distance service (hauled by "Britannia" Pacific No. 70046) called at Stoke in emergency to set down two passengers (probably due to the cancellation of a preceding train). This service ended in 1966, which meant the end of all steam passenger trains calling at or passing through Stoke Mandeville.

As mentioned earlier, London Transport had been in charge of engineering work on the line since 1948, and it continued to carry out many maintenance tasks almost to the end of the period being described. London Transport engineers' trains which sometimes called at or near Stoke continued to run until about the winter of 1966/7, the last one seen by the writer being hauled by pannier-tank No. L.93 on 5th. October 1966. The unmistakable sound of a pannier was also heard twice during the small hours of 22nd. January 1967, but as the trains were not seen, their visit(s) must remain unconfirmed. The very last steam train to pass through Stoke Mandeville in normal service would have been one of these LT engineers' trains, not counting any special trains organised during the pleasant steam revival of recent years.

Before nationalisation the two partners, LT and the LNER had kept strictly to their own sphere of influence, despite the fact that the line was administered by their joint committee. However after 1961 the line seemed more 'joint' than ever before. For instance, on 25th. July 1965 an LT engineer's train hauled by L.95 and laden with sleepers ran through Stoke to Aylesbury and back, and at the same time a BR (LMR) train hauled by a diesel loco, was engaged on embankment repairs near Stoke Mandeville Hospital.

The full service of diesel trains which began in 1962 continued for nearly three decades, the main changes being in the livery of the carriages, which chameleon-like appeared successively in dark green, all blue, blue and grey and in the red, white and blue of recent liveries which are patriotic if not to everybody's taste. Recently Stoke has been facelifted under the Chiltern Line refurbishment, and today sees a service of the splendid new Turbo trains.

THE STOKE MANDEVILLE 'LINESCAPE'

In 1948 Stoke Mandeville was a station newly acquired by London Transport and thus technically part of the Underground. What did it look like? The main building looked very much as it does today except as regards finish or lack of it. A similar set of facilities, rather fewer in number, stood on the opposite platform. The goods yard was on the site of the present car park. Just within the yard stood a small weighbridge office for the weighing of lorries, and further in was a tall building of corrugated iron used in later years to store artificial fertilisers. It had doors opening on to the track and the roadway. At each end of the one siding in the yard was a set of buffer stops. Each consisted of a framework of old rails, and the "beam" (literally a beam in early examples) was made of three lengths of rail. Where the frames were painted they were black, but the "beams" were soon painted bright red with conspicuous white ends, a characteristic London Transport feature, maintained for years after LT had relinquished responsibility as far as the public was concerned. The iron chairs into which the rails were fitted and which were fixed to the sleepers, showed some interesting origins by the lettering embossed upon them, variously:

GWR 1902MET RLY 1931/2
MET & GC 1910LNE-C 1944.
GCR 1913

Between the passenger platforms some of the sleepers were later fitted with standard London Transport plates in black-on-white enamel indicating where trains of differing lengths should come to a stand. An interesting variety of miniature disc signals (or "dollies") guarded the various points. A loading gauge was suspended over the goods yard track to regulate the height to which wagons might be laden: it was felled in February 1961. Across the tracks stood the attractive Met. signal box, opened as required to deal with freight traffic. Signals (other than miniatures) were limited to the following: a home and a distant signal, both colour-lights, situated north of the station and applying to trains approaching from the Aylesbury direction; the distant signal controlling trains from London which had a modern LNER upper quadrant enamel arm, and its home counterpart which had a wooden Great Central arm. Both were on concrete posts. No starting signal was provided at the London-bound platform, but that for the other direction had a GCR wooden post surmounted by a ball-and-spike finial. In wartime days the LNER had covered everything that did not move with a coat of austerity matt grey, including most of the Stoke structures already mentioned. By 1948 the whole premises gave a sad impression, though the gloom was relieved by many shiny enamel signs with white letters on an ultramarine background. These included posterboard headings variously lettered in Gill Sans style "LONDON TRANSPORT", "LONDON AND NORTH EASTERN RAILWAY" or a contraction of one or both titles; they were all, however, provided by the LNER. On the doors too similar plates appeared – "WAITING ROOM" for example, in the "Grotesque" style of lettering used by the Metropolitan and probably original. More blue signs at the platform ends cautioned passengers against crossing the line. The night-time gloom on the platforms was barely relieved at all, as only hurricane lamps marked the platform ends. A touch of colour was given by "temporary" paper placards bearing the station name on the well-known LT ring-and-bar symbol, which had been pasted to boards erected on posts some years previously. These LT signs supplemented what appeared to be the original Met. Railway nameboards, very large with letters about a foot high. Enamelled in the standard blue, they had been taken down in the war to reappear after hostilities with a painted background of grey. A few enamel signs hanging under the canopy – "WAY OUT" and so on – had been shakily overpainted on to a black background. Large boards bearing the station's name in screwed-on metal letters were fixed to each end of the signal box. Their last repaint by the LNER had been in white on black.

The above state of affairs lasted until 1950, when London Transport began a series of improvements. The first installation to be overhauled was the station lighting. New electric lamps appeared under the footbridge canopy and in some rooms, while lighting was freshly installed along the platforms. Not electric, however, but some of the ancient oil lamps were renovated and fitted to creosoted posts. Of pleasing design, some had the station name displayed in black letters engraved on translucent white glass panels. Their amber glow was entertaining if not illuminating. In 1952 London Transport undertook a complete renovation of the station buildings, together with those at Wendover and Great Missenden. Undersides of canopies were painted cream, and the upper half of supporting pillars was a fresh pale green. However almost all the remaining paintwork was finished in a sombre dark brown, even including the copiously-wooded window frames. From the station approach the view was rather forbidding, as the grim dark brown hardly contrasted with the grimy yellow brickwork. The "temporary" nameplates persisted, but the old large nameboards were discarded. A little further brightness was added by standard LT enamel signs as fitted to more modern stations, which replaced the old door-plates. It was interesting at the time to see how the new owners would deal with the old raised-letter signs (signal box, "PRIVATE ROAD" and trespass) bequeathed by the LNER which did not feature in the LT scheme of things. They played safe, and finished them all exactly as the LNER had, with white letters on a black ground. Other splashes of colour were new standard red signs at the platform ends warning passengers not to proceed beyond that point. An amusing line was that addressed to staff – "DO NOT STEP ON ANY RAIL" – the nearest electrified track was still 18.51 miles away at Rickmansworth!

The diagonally-planked fencing, possibly of LNER origin, was retained along both platforms and is still in place today. Until the very recent refurbishment there was a wide gate in the fencing at the London end of the up platform which in earlier days allowed road vehicles to load or unload directly on to the platform. Along the platforms bench-seats were placed, and judging by photographic evidence may have dated from the early days of the line and be of Metropolitan origin. Of neat, modern-looking design, the actual seat was a single wide plank, two other planks forming a backrest. Iron "legs", grouped in pairs in a single casting were fitted one at each end and one centrally. In early days the station name had been displayed along the top backrest in screwed-on iron letters. During the 1952 renovations these letters were laboriously chiselled off. At one time Stoke boasted about 10 of these seats, but they were gradually replaced by ones of modern style, shorter but not dissimilar, by the LMR in 1967. The last "original" seat did not disappear until the recent refurbishment, by which time it had received a new seat-plank and was painted bright blue. The seats had usually been one colour all over and received the almost universal dark brown in 1952 but in later years were black.

Very prominent on the London-bound platform in 1948 was a wooden structure with a pitched roof covering the station well. It had a very large iron wheel, and I last saw water being drawn by a member of staff about 1951. During the LT renovations a year later the structure was demolished and the site of the well covered by an inspection plate. This small "well-house" would have been a good candidate for preservation had the interest in railwayana existed at that time! Parked in various parts of the station one could always see a few luggage trolleys and porter's barrows, provided by the ER or LMR depending on the period. They were usually finished in one of the current building colours.

In 1953 London Transport undertook a general renovation of signals, carrying out a very thorough and painstaking job. All posts were finished "silver" (aluminium), and high quality red, yellow, white and black paint was used on semaphore arms and other components.

A few years later it was announced that the Met. line was to be completely modernised, equipped with new trains and curtailed at Amersham. Stoke did not alter much in appearance for some time although a few changes – slewing of the siding, resiting of the two platelayers' huts to allow platform lengthening for example – were seen over the next few years. By August 1961 as the day approached for the old order of train services to change, London Transport re-renovated the signal boxes and signals on the line. Stoke box was repainted as before – all dark brown with cream eaves and window frames – but the black background to the nameboards was missing; they were simply finished in the body brown. This suggested a rushed job, as only the next month the shortening of the Met. line occurred, and the Amersham – Aylesbury section, including Stoke of course, went over to BR London Midland Region cosmetically at least. The signals were repainted much as before, mainly silver but with fewer black trimmings, and were again repainted from November 1963 onwards by the LMR, this time in a white-and-black scheme (dollies all black) with red and yellow components as appropriate. The "temporary" nameboards in use since about 1944 were overpasted with new really temporary paper sheets bearing the name on the BR "totem" or "double-sausage" logo in regional maroon. A few maroon enamel signs also appeared – "TICKETS" being one of the first. The LMR's signal and telegraph department also assumed responsibility for the signalling system. Far from relinquishing entire control of the premises though, London Transport continued to deal with track maintenance among other things for some five years more. Following the partial takeover by the LMR in 1961 the Stoke Mandeville east-side buildings were given their second redecoration by LT, ten years after the first. The scheme was unique, and quite different from that used at Wendover and Great Missenden. Stoke's canopy was painted a pleasant light buff, and platform pillars were an attractive grey-blue; doors were navy blue and window frames were cream. Against these hues the dark red of the BR signs, which were all in place by the end of 1962, stood out well. The west-side buildings were not so fortunate, being condemned. By early 1964 they were a heap of rubble, and their site was soon marked by only a patch of newer tarmac. Their place was rather inadequately taken by August 1964 by a wooden shelter like those common on London Transport country bus routes. It survived until the Chiltern Line refurbishment.

Despite its repaint only two years earlier, the signal box was again repainted. In the interval London Transport had gone modern with its colours, and this time the box was painted light grey with cream windows and black doors. The nameboards were painted in the grey body-colour of the box, upon which the white lettering did not show up at all well. In theory they should have been maroon as befits an LMR structure, and as regional colours were abandoned a few years later, the boards at Stoke went right through the LMR's "maroon" period without receiving a coat of that colour.

During the later fifties the existing oil and electric lights of the main building (where some rooms were still devoid of any artificial lighting) were supplemented by gas lamps in the toilets, cycle-room and under the porch canopy. Along the platforms the original oil lamp casings were replaced in May 1960 by "new" ones which, judging by their blue paint, were re-used gas lamps from Chorley Wood, which had recently converted to electricity. By September 1963 all the oil lamp casings were fitted with pressure lamps complete with mantles, but they were gradually left unused. In December 1964 the first electric strip-light was switched into use, and strings of temporary tungsten lamps were draped along the platform fences. The oil lamps were finally removed in February 1965, and in mid-summer that year grey-painted steel columns bearing fluorescent lights were erected along the platforms. New strip-lights were hung beneath the platform canopies, their shades bearing the station name in the new BR alphabet.

As part of the 1963 repaint the goods yard buildings also received attention. The weighbridge office was finished in the navy/cream/black scheme applied to the main buildings, and the goods shed was a medium grey all over. The weighbridge office only lasted until the Christmas period of 1964 however, as the site of much of the yard was bulldozed for a new car park, later extended. The yard was officially closed on 5th. July 1965, and the associated signalling was taken out of use on 1st. May 1966. Two years later the siding was lifted, and in 1969 the box was dismantled. In the ashes of the nearby bonfire, the charred remains of a Metropolitan Railway document relating to the conveyance of hay were found: it was dated 1905! After withdrawal of LT from the scene, the station became purely British Railways (London Midland Region) and remained so until taken over in turn by the Western Region, Network SouthEast and Chiltern Railways.

The station footbridge changed very little over the years apart from the fitting of an asbestos roof in place of the previous corrugated iron in 1950 and certain minor strengthenings. It had always been finished in the general station colour-scheme, but London Transport introduced a blue-grey hue said to have been voted for by a panel of suburban residents as a colour that did not stand out too obtrusively against a sky background. Thereafter this scheme was used for most LT bridges on steelwork and wooden parts alike. It was also used on the nearby bridge carrying Station Road.

Bridges, tunnels and culverts were fitted with number-plates of Metropolitan Railway design originally. They were of oblong shape with incurved corners bearing the number below the smaller initials "M R". The two station bridges were numbers 152 & 153, the numbering sequence having started at the Baker Street tunnels. While LT was still in charge of maintenance in 1964 these Met. plates were supplemented by a new design of its own, narrower oblongs with rounded corners. Happily the old company initials were perpetuated, thirty-one years after the Metropolitan ceased to exist!

Distances were also measured from Baker Street, and until recently an early Met. Railway milepost stood by the roadbridge at the north end of the Aylesbury-bound platform. Its triangular-section wooden head showed that it was set 36 miles from Baker Street. Other posts up the line had long ago received screwed-on metal numbers or had been completely replaced by previous owners using cast iron or concrete posts, but our ancient sign had to be signwritten on its flush surfaces. In the period 1948-1968, it was painted white (later yellow) with black characters, and it was only removed in 1991 when a new fibreglass sign was erected across the track – again numbered 36 although LT had long gone metric for posts on its section of line nearer London.

Gradient posts were long a trackside feature in the days of loose-coupled goods trains, and one was installed just on the Aylesbury side of Stoke's roadbridge. The history of these posts and their replacements was much the same as that of the mileposts and again Stoke's specimen was a very early one, its arms having to be handpainted with precision. One arm indicated that the slope towards Aylesbury at that point was 1 in 117, while that in the Wendover direction was 1 in 264. This sign was purchased by the writer in 1992 and presented to Quainton's museum.

For most of the period, publicity at street level was nil, so both the goods yard and passenger station were completely anonymous. Until late years a cast iron sign (headed with the joint committee's title, but believed to be of Met. Railway origin), stood in the station approach indicating that it was a private road, but the name of the station was not displayed until the LMR arrived on the scene. Then a set of posterboards was installed facing the main road, which were surmounted by a "STOKE MANDEVILLE STATION" sign flanked by BR totems in the current dark red and white enamel.

At the beginning of the period a traditional tarred sleeper-built hut with roses round the door stood in the goods yard. It was soon replaced by the concrete structures which were erected at the south end of the down platform. These seemed to be of Southern Region origin, even to the extent of having grass-green paintwork. The larger hut was eventually replaced in turn by one similar to a creosoted garden-shed which lasted throughout the period.

Finally, mention must be made of the station gardens for which Stoke Mandeville has long been well-known. Roses of the Paul's Scarlet and Alexandra varieties grew along the platform fence, and were lovingly tended by Messrs. Allen and Spittles, and when the gardens won the London Transport All Lines competition in the mid-fifties the Chairman declared the display of marigolds one of the best he had ever seen. A huge freely-fruiting grapevine grew on the south wall of the station buildings, though sadly this has lately been refurbished out. Less in the public eye were supplies of onions yielded by an allotment which a member of staff tended near the signal box. These were destined for Stoke Mandeville Hospital and were stored prior to dispatch in the goods shed.

Stoke Mandeville station as seen from the northbound platform on 3rd. August 1959 when the station was under the control of London Transport. Each platform has its own set of offices. They have small signs (e.g., "WAITING ROOM") affixed at right angles to the wall. They are in black or blue on white with or without a red ring. A Metropolitan Line train from Aylesbury approaches.

STOKE MANDEVILLE

PHOTOGRAPHS

Winter 1962–63

A view of the station on the 3rd. May 1964, looking bright in its final repaint by London Transport. The 'gibbet' on the right bore no fittings; possibly it was designed to hold a lamp.

Seen from under the canopy of the recently-refurbished station, Standard Class 5 locomotive No. 73031 passes the colourful garden with a Nottingham train on 29th. July 1965.

By 7th. June 1965 the old northbound buildings had been replaced by what appears to be a standard London Transport country bus shelter. The footbridge is in LT bridge blue-grey overall. Temporary electric lighting dangles above the platform and totems have been fixed to the fencing.

The station porch after renovation by LT when the station was publicly an LMR property. The white-framed poster-boards with an inner black border are a typical LT feature of the time. The middle-aged gas lamp still hangs under the canopy which is rather unusually painted navy blue to match the doors. 29th. November 1964.

Seen across the yellow brick rubble of the far platform buildings, 'Black Five' 4-6-0 No. 45215 passes through Stoke on a morning train from Nottingham on 25th. January 1964.

135

One of the standard oil lamps with the translucent name-panel still showing traces of wartime blackout paint, photographed about 1953. Compare with preserved example on Page 94.

Most of the oil lamps had lost their name-panel by the time they were reinstated by LT in 1950 as shown (photographed on 3rd. August 1959). Each surmounted a paper station name sign stuck on to an asbestos sheet. The oil vessel made sure that none of the negligible light reached the placard below! Part of Mr. Sanderson's prize-winning garden may be seen.

Changing lights: on 30th. January 1965 this fluorescent lamp had recently supplanted the gas lamp just behind – which had gone a week later.

136

ABOVE: During THAT winter of 1962-3, this shot was taken on 7th. January and shows one of several ex-gas lamps believed to have come from Chorley Wood, recently converted to electricity. Beneath the snow an ex-Met. Railway bench lies hidden.
ABOVE RIGHT: This photograph was taken from the same spot on 5th. September 1967 when fluorescent lights had replaced oil. The Met. seat is now revealed.

Steam billows from under bridge No. MR 153 as LT 0-6-0PT No. L.90 bursts out with a permanent way train from the Aylesbury direction very early on the morning of 19th. June 1966. The station is under LMR control as far as the public is concerned – note the dark red nameboard – but London Transport is still undertaking track maintenance. The bridge is starkly modern for an 1892 design.

137

Photographed again minutes later, No. L.90 – LT's second ex-GWR pannier tank to bear this number – now simmers at the platform before returning to Neasden Depot. The leading brake-van, B.584, has recently been repainted in standard LT colours with mid grey sides, bus red ends and black underframes. It is of BR standard type based on an LNER design. A group of permanent way men are gathered on the veranda. See also photograph on page 57.

The indeterminate position of the signal-arm does not confuse the driver of D3796 as the train laden with sand is backing away from the camera. It is working "wrong road" during work on an embankment-slip near Stoke Mandeville Hospital. The signal was bought by a local enthusiast and later presented to the National Railway Museum. 13th. March 1966.

The view south towards Wendover on 3rd. August 1959. The LT SR-style concrete hut and the wooden one of unknown parentage to the right, the rubbish pit and the LNER buffer-stops have yet to be moved and the siding slewed to allow platform lengthening in readiness for 8-car trains. The goods shed may be seen on the left with a few trucks beyond near the loading-gauge. The Met. signal-box with its LNER nameboard stands across the track, but the nearby home signal is lost against the line of lofty elms so characteristic of the district at that time.

ABOVE LEFT: The simple goods shed, all over grey, on 7th. June 1965. ABOVE RIGHT: The weighbridge office on 3rd. January 1965 during the last year of the yard's operation. The door is navy, other woodwork cream and the pipes are black. The weighbridge itself has already been removed.

139

Some of the last wagons and coal stocks to be brought to the yard are seen on 7th. June 1965, a month before closure. The wagon numbers are B 101359, B 181312 and B 588535.

The view south on 3rd. May 1964. One of the goods yard gates finished in LT bridge-grey may be seen, and beyond them the lengthened platforms may just be discerned.

The date is 1st. June 1968 and the goods yard has become a car park. British Rail's new alphabet is used for
the signs mainly in black on white, with red highlights.

140

Back on the platform for a moment, here we have the station well-house on 27th. December 1952. Still in the remains of LNER wartime grey with black ironwork, it was soon removed. The cables in the background fixed to telegraph-pole 30 led into a metal box initialled LER (London Electric Railway)!

One of the standard maroon totems affixed to the fence after the LMR take-over. At LT's first general repaint in 1952 the old GCR sign was finished in LNER style – white on black with a station brown post, but is seen here as repainted by them in 1955 with colours reversed. The post remains brown. The sign and the brick-built rubbish bunker were formerly at the platform end, but have now been bypassed by the platforms, extended to accommodate the longer diesel trains. 7th. January 1963.

141

From this view taken on 7th. June 1965 one can see that the buffer-stops have again been removed – by several runaway wagons during some exuberant shunting.

It is 6th. August 1965, and No. 9T02 goods rumbles through Stoke hauled by Standard 2-6-0 No. 76035. It will not call, as Stoke yard has been closed for a month. The red buffer-beam with meticulously-painted white ends is a typical LT finish. With its back to us in the foreground is the by then unique GCR disc-signal controlling entry to the yard from the London direction.

The wide farm-crossing to the south of the goods yard, with vehicular and pedestrian gates. The concrete post used to bear a pair of joint committee signs in cast iron, warning users against trespass and danger. Photographed on 4th. June 1982.

The pedestrian gate on the west side of the same crossing. The farmer had been told that it was erected in 1904. It is certainly of great antiquity and bears more than traces of what appears to be GCR buff paint. It still survives at the time of writing.

ABOVE LEFT: Mr. Alfred Sanderson stands in his LT uniform on the signal box balcony on 25th. August 1958. The box is in all over LT 1952 dark brown, relieved only by cream window frames and eaves; its LNER nameboard is white on black. Mr. Sanderson had recently won the London Transport All Lines station gardens competition.

ABOVE RIGHT: The signal box after its final repaint by LT in light grey with ivory window frames and black doors. The nameboard is not easily legible with its grey background. 1st. February 1964.

The down home signal alongside BR standard milepost 35¾. It has a GCR arm upon an unpainted concrete post. It is undated, but similar ones on the line bore the date 1918. The counter-balance weight is marked "LNE-C 30". The signal was normally kept at 'clear' unless a goods train was due to call, or single-line working was in progress due to engineering work. The corresponding distant signal nearer to Wendover also had a concrete post with an LNER upper quadrant arm dated 1938. Photographed 29th. July 1965.

The GCR starting signal at danger during permanent way work on 25th. July 1965. The post has been repainted black and white by the LMR in place of LT silver. By this time the wooden Met. milepost has lost the "M" that used to surmount the numerals. A standard dark red LMR sign guards the platform end. The girders of the road-bridge are in LT bridge grey.

Since the photo on Page 107 was taken this Saxby & Farmer signal has been painted black by the LMR. This design was once common on the line, their cheerful faces shining out in some quantity in Aylesbury goods yard, for instance. The whole lantern revolves at right angles to show a green light. The danger aspect shows a white light. From wartime days onwards some were replaced by LNER standard signals where the disc, with a horizontal red stripe, revolved in the vertical plane to display a diagonal stripe and a green light. One of these controlled the crossover from the up to the down road between the platforms. It was generally similar to the type shown in the next picture. 13th. November 1965.

145

This disc-signal was put in about 1951 and is of a later Metropolitan Rly. type; the disc is fixed to a simple fitting instead of a complete semaphore arm. The post bears the initials of the Westinghouse Brake and Saxby Signal Company. When photographed on 11th. August 1966 it no longer guarded the crossover from the down to the up road as on Page 139 but was standing at the platform end awaiting collection as scrap.

Another ex-Met Railway disc-signal of the earlier type with a miniature arm to which the disc is bolted. Although the signal governs the exit from the yard on to the up running line neither the disc nor the arm have a red glass – neither is there a lamp. The signal bears the name "MET RLY", and is in overall LMR black except for the anonymous white-painted 28lb. weight. Photographed on 7th. April 1966.

This signal was made up from parts of two of the identical Met. signals after they had been withdrawn. The disc has been removed and the arm displays the part number SD 163, but unlike the post, no company name; it is believed to be older. The signal is destined for an East Anglian railway museum.

Boards similar to this one were used at Stoke Mandeville until the LMR takeover. They differed slightly from this preserved example as when in earlier days the background was left in natural grey asbestos, the blue bar had an inner lining of white. When the bar was plain blue as here the whole background was covered with white paper.

Two typical LNER notice-board headings removed from Stoke when LT took over – the boards were then left unheaded. The plates are in dark blue enamel with white lettering, which refers to the origin of the posters beneath, not to the provider of the plates. As a further example, some of these LNER plates at Aylesbury were lettered GWR, as the boards bore that company's posters.

ABOVE LEFT: Despite bearing the initials of the Metropolitan Railway, this bridge plate (fixed on the parapet in Station Road) was provided in 1964, thirty years after the Met.'s demise! "MR" was still the official prefix to Metropolitan Line bridge numbers. The provision of these 'permanent' signs at this late date was surprising as the line was already LMR property and LT would disappear from the scene altogether within a few years. The plate itself proved to be not so permanent as it disappeared in turn during 1970. It is white on black, and the photograph was taken on 8th. November 1964.

ABOVE RIGHT: An all-wooden gradient post believed to be of Met. Railway design and one of a few survivors on the line. It is well protected from the elements by Station Road bridge. Examples remaining on former Met. territory already under London Transport had long ago received screwed-on metal letters to aid painters, but these few on the ex-GCR/LNER section still had to be carefully signwritten. 12th. April 1971.

Although just over the boundary in Wendover this LNER standard mile post represents the few in Stoke Mandeville parish. They had an iron head on a concrete post, and appeared at 35½, 36¼ and 36½ miles from Baker Street. On these the fraction only appeared. It will be seen on milepost 35 that although the top is comparatively small, the neat characters are very legible. The dark tone is due to the post having been painted yellow by the LMR by the time it was photographed on 17th. August 1982.

By contrast, this old Met. mile post has a wooden head on a post of old rail. Like the gradient post on Page 148 it has to be sign-written, not always consistently executed as regards size and style of characters. This post is also in LMR yellow and was photographed on 12th. April 1971. The Station Road bridge plate, a genuine Met. Railway specimen has MR 153 in black and white. Earlier, LT used either the same combination or with colours reversed. This plate also disappeared soon after being photographed.

This LNER "CATCH POINTS" sign was provided just north of the Station Road bridge. Catch points were designed to trap runaway wagons and turn them off the track instead of gathering speed down the gradient towards Aylesbury. The black post is typical of LMR painting. It was photographed on 24th. May 1971.

A pair of warning signs like this was provided at each side of the line at pedestrian and vehicular crossings. Although this pair, photographed on 21st. April 1971 is just in Wendover parish it is typical of those at Stoke's two crossings, a farm-crossing shown on Page 143 and one for pedestrians near milepost 36½. The lower plate is a GCR design common on the line north of Great Missenden, but the upper one is unique to the Stoke Mandeville area. The 'chunky' lettering employed was usually reserved for much larger plates. All the pairs in Stoke were identical except those at the pedestrian crossing where the lower signs were of different pattern. They warned trespassers that the penalty was 40 shilling (sic), and although of generally GCR design were one of the few types to be seen both on the Met./LT and GCR/LNER sections.

A black-on-white plate which had been affixed to the signal box door, and warned against unauthorised entry. It is signed by John Bell, managing director of the Met. Railway. It is accompanied by an "Adlake" oil-lamp as used on local signals. Although this one has an LNER plate on the back the type was very common right up the line.

Demolition of the building on the down platform at Stoke Mandeville. 18th. January 1964.

APPENDIX 1.
EPHEMERA

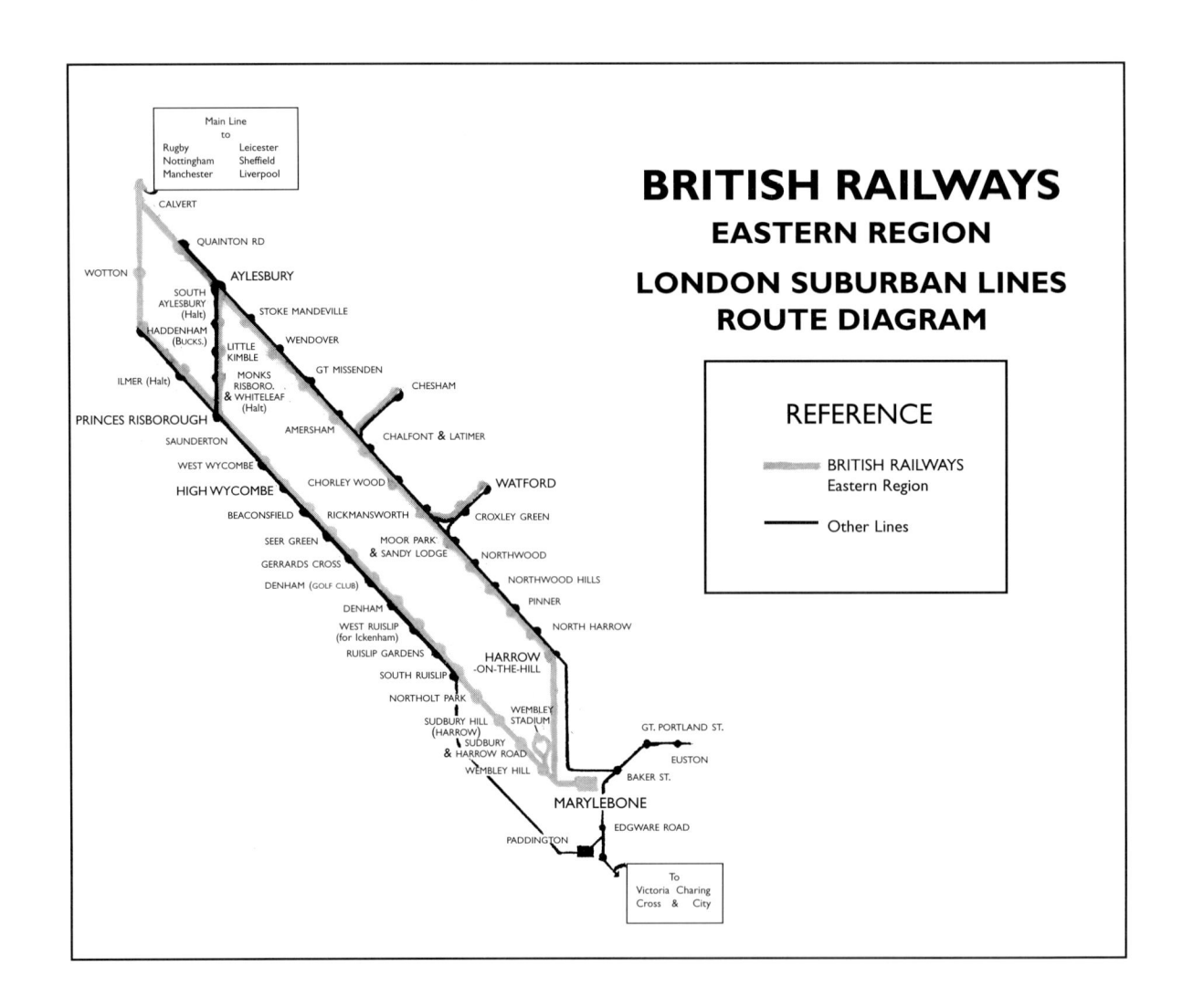

[A] A 1948 timetable booklet still showed Quainton Road as jointly served.

[B] Part of a Met. Railway form in stock at Willesden Green in 1959.

[C] Newspapers by Underground: a label.

> EVENING STANDARD PER LONDON TRANSPORT CONTRACT
> EVENING STANDARD AGENT
>
> BAKER ST   HARROW.ON.THE HILL

[D] Part of an LT/BR handout.

> BRITISH RAIL   LONDON TRANSPORT
>
> MESSAGE TO TRAVELLERS   14 October 1981
>
> AUTUMN LEAVES
>
> With this year's leaf fall nearly with us, we are taking the opportunity of telling you what has been planned by London Transport and British Rail to overcome this annual problem on the joint LT/BR line from Baker Street and Marylebone to Amersham and Aylesbury. We are optimistic that an improvement in reliability and punctuality will be achieved with our services on the line this autumn as a result of the measures being taken.
>
> *Sandite

[E] Preservation paperwork.

> PURCHASER'S COPY
>
> LONDON TRANSPORT EXECUTIVE
> DESPATCH NOTE   B 80118
>
> FROM Stoke Mandeville Station   TO A.J. Reed Esq
>   Nightingale Rd
>   Southcourt
>   Aylesbury Bucks
>
> DATE 28 January 1958 SALES CONTRACT NUMBER Cash   DELIVERY NUMBER
> TRUCK NUMBER   ORDER   CARRIER   CARRIAGE
>
> | Package No. | List No. | Description | Quan. | Weight (Tons/cwt/qr/lb) | Rate | Amount (£/s/d) |
> |---|---|---|---|---|---|---|
> | | | Redundant Oil Lamp | 1 | | | 2 6 |

153

[F] Part of an LPTB Metropolitan Line goods invoice in stock at Willesden Green in 1959.

[G] Part of a timetable compiler's chart (above) shows that LT still had an interest in Quainton Road at that time.

Warning of noise on railway

BECAUSE of further essential maintenance work to be carried out on the railway tracks between Aylesbury and Amersham, London Transport point out that a ballast tamping machine will again be used and some noise will be unavoidable.

Work will start at night between Amersham and Great Missenden from Tuesday until October 10 and will continue between Great Missenden and Wendover from October 13 until the 17th; north and south of Wendover from the 19th to the 24th; between Stoke Mandeville and Aylesbury from the 27th until the 29th and between Wendover and Stoke Mandeville from the 30th until the 31st.

Noisy nights ahead

London Transport has apologised in advance to people living near the Aylesbury-Marylebone line between Great Missenden and Wendover, who may be disturbed by all-night maintenance work to be carried out on the line.

Noisy nights are to be from February 23 to February 26 inclusive. London Transport is undertaking the maintenance work on behalf of British Rail's Midland Region.

[H] Local press notices warning of night-time noise during the 'LT/BR joint' period after 1961. 12th. February and 25th. September 1964.

[I] Part of a document discarded on demolition of Stoke signal box. Dated 29th. March 1905, the message reads: "From Strong to S. Keyes. Our invoice 752 of yesterday F. Mead 100 trusses hay 19s. 7 paid Should be to pay note and collect". It was telegraphed to F by CB at 4.32 p.m.

[J] A lineside photographic permit issued to the author. Note the inclusion of Winslow Road, closed nearly 30 years earlier!

155

APPENDIX 2.
METROPOLITAN RAILWAY TRANSFERS

NUMERALS UNCOVERED ON DOOR OF COACH NO. 212 AT AYLESBURY, 1967 © A.J.R.

DOOR NUMERAL (OUTSIDE)
ACTUAL SIZE

FIGURES FROM GARNISH RAIL (INSIDE)
ACTUAL SIZE
Unedged gilt, shaded black

KEY TO COLOURS

- (1) DARK BLUE, SLIGHTLY GREYISH, APPROX. HUMBROL 15
- (2) DOTS OF (1) ON BACKGROUND OF (3)
- (3) MID BLUE, AS (1) WITH ADDED WHITE
- (4) DOTS OF (3) ON BACKGROUND OF (5)
- (5) PALE BLUE-GREY

Number gilt, shadow black. Whole outlined with black approx. 0.5mm in thickness. Bands of colour had hard edges but no outline.

continued on next page

The garnish rail transfers shown on Page 156 were also used on Dreadnought stock and could be seen until 1951 when doors were painted plain brown and standard LT numerals were applied. Previously the old Met. style transfers were not renewed but were repeatedly revarnished at each repaint of the coach, so that latterly they shone through the varnish with a deep amber glow. Class numerals on the inside of No.212's doors were taller than the external ones – 7¾″ × 6″ overall. They had been overpainted in unedged deep cream with black shading; there was no trace of the original colour.

Third class open: the end of Met. coach No. 212, 1967.

THE END

– not of a mediaeval barn but of Great Missenden goods shed. Having survived throughout our period it was being demolished on 6th. June 1969 ...

... and of Class F 0-6-2T No. L.50, being cut up at Neasden Depot on 15th. March 1959, with the help of crane No. C.604.